ENDORSI

This is not your grandparent's generation leadership book; not even another voice in the long line of leadership theory or research. Rather, it is the powerfully personable stories of what makes leaders authentic, productive, and able to redeem any circumstance into teachable moments to serve others. Felicia Linch has delivered what is needed to wake us up to the real and raw lessons we must all process and embrace to become the best versions of our leadership selves for the world.

- **Dr. Joseph Umidi, Founder & CEO, Lifeforming Leadership Coaching**

Tremendous! This book is tremendous. It gave me all the feels and I could not put it down. It is one of the books that engrossed me and then gave me hope. It was honest and practical . . . with a good sprinkle of faith. I learned so much, including the importance of seeing the best in others.

- **Gillian Rowe, author, director of Lex Nova Core, and co-founder of Read for Life Barbados**

Bravo! A real live human leader! This book is unique among leadership books in that it doesn't give you a list of principles or qualities in theory. Felicia Linch, in complete alignment with what she believes about leadership, chooses to be 100% vulnerable by sharing the raw material of her own fumbling and victorious journey into an authentic and powerful leader. She exposes all the false notions of what we think it means to be a leader, the shallow buzzwords we throw around but rarely see exhibited, and the common paths to incomplete and inadequate transformation of the inner leader. The world must have leaders today who have seen and mastered their own inner life. Apart from that, they are not equipped to bring transformation to a world that desperately needs it at every turn. The world has found one such leader in Felicia. I hope this book multiplies many more!

- Tricia Exman, coach, communicator, catalyst, and owner of Presence Coaching

THE INVISIBLE LEADER
STEPPING UP, STEPPING OUT

FELICIA LINCH

urbanpress

The Invisible Leader
by Felicia Linch
Copyright © 2019 Felicia Linch

ISBN # 978-1-63360-128-4

All rights reserved under International Copyright Law. Written permission must be secured from the publisher/author to reproduce, copy, or transmit any part of this book.

Unless otherwise noted, all scripture quotations taken from the Holy Bible, New International Version®, NIV®. Copyright © 1973, 1978, 1984, 2011 by Biblica, Inc.™ Used by permission of Zondervan. All rights reserved worldwide. www.zondervan.com The "NIV" and "New International Version" are trademarks registered in the United States Patent and Trademark Office by Biblica, Inc.

For Worldwide Distribution Printed in the U.S.A.

Urban Press
P.O. Box 8881
Pittsburgh, PA 15221-0881 USA
412.646.2780
www.urbanpress.us

TABLE OF CONTENTS

Introduction	xi
Chapter 1: Leaders Don't Fail: Failing Forward	1
Chapter 2: Turning the Corner: Finding the Courage to Move Forward	13
Chapter 3: Purposed for Leadership: The Journey to Self-Awareness	21
Chapter 4: Leadership: What Does It Take?	35
Chapter 5: Labels: It's All about Identity	47
Chapter 6: Do I Really Have to Serve?	55
Chapter 7: Holding Others Accountable: Finding the Balance	71
Concluding Thoughts	81
Felicia Linch, MBA, CIPD, LLB	87

ACKNOWLEDGEMENTS

This book has been a journey and I thank Holy Spirit for guiding me through it and enabling me to see myself. I also want to thank the following people, who have not only supported me in bringing this book to fruition but have also helped shape the leader I'm becoming:

To my family: my husband Andrew who has walked this journey with me, enduring much personal sacrifice that no one could imagine; my dad, Godfrey Oranye, who pushed me to be and do the best, even when at times I thought he was being too hard. As an adult I can now say I am truly grateful that you pushed; my mum, Gloria, O for her unwavering love, even when she didn't agree with and could understand the choices I made; my brother Ore and sisters Chineze and Chinwe—your love, support, and wisdom have been invaluable, but more than that, I value our friendship and would choose those friendships even if we weren't related!

To the many mentors and coaches I have been blessed to have: Dr. Julian Laite, Dr. John Stanko, Lyn Eichmann, Dr. Joseph Umidi (where I first learned about support, encouragement, and accountability), and Jenni Catron. Thank you all for modeling leadership and for helping me to grow.

To my church family: Pastor Don Cousins and all the leaders who God used throughout the course of this book to bring clarification and a solid foundation to what Holy Spirit was showing me, and to my Mid-week Reflections group who help keep me accountable.

Lastly, to all my friends, Mobola Aguda, Liza Bynoe, Marsha Lewis, Monique Hassell, Jeanette Charles, Lynn Eichmann, Martha Collett, Margaret Johnson, Brian and Barton King, and Tricia Examan, and so many others too numerous to mention. You have all taught me something and I value your honesty even when sharing with me the things I may not have wanted but needed to hear and without which I would not be the leader I am today.

Thank you to everyone. I love you all very much!

DEDICATION

To Cislyn Spence—I am so grateful for
the reflection of Jesus you were to me, showing me
what a life of purpose in Him looks like.
Eternally grateful to you and the Holy Spirit!

INTRODUCTION
WHY ANOTHER LEADERSHIP BOOK?

You may have groaned when you saw yet another book on leadership, and, if you did, I would not blame you. There are a ton of books on the topic, all with varying philosophies and approaches. That being said, you may ask: Why is she writing a book to add to the collection?

I am doing this because as a consultant who helps governments and corporations undertake large-scale transformation programmes, I've found that the greatest fundamental challenge to successful transformation—be it of nations, organisations, or self—is leadership.

A 2013 *Forbes* magazine article, entitled the "Crisis of Leadership," reported that 86% of respondents to a 2015

World Economic Forum Global Agenda Survey agreed that there is a leadership crisis in the world today. Similarly, a 2017 *Huffington Post* article spoke of the "Global Crisis of Leadership," stating:

> Yes, leaders are a reflection of their time, and people the world over might have finally reached the breaking point. Their cry for trusting, caring, and bold leadership echoes everywhere. We can only hope that such leaders will hear the people's outcry and emerge to answer their desperate call.[1]

I am of the view that *all* people are purposed for leadership. In fact, I almost titled this book *Purposed for Leadership*. By that phrase, I am not referring to people who may be considered "natural-born leaders" because of their charismatic leadership style or persuasive communication skills. We all know people who seem naturally comfortable, even at a young age, while they are leading and influencing others—for good or bad.

Being purposed for leadership is more than this, however. It manifests itself when someone has an innate sense of wanting to achieve a goal or purpose bigger than they are for the benefit of others. As Robert Greenleaf put it, it's a focus on serving first and then a conscious choice to lead.

Yet many people who *are* purposed for leadership either don't know it or have been running away from the assignment. They have become what I call invisible leaders because they have either made themselves invisible due to fear or cultural restrictions, or are invisible to others due to racial, gender, or cultural bias. Today, the world needs effective leaders of character, for the challenges of our world can no longer be solved with the ideas and approaches of the past. In these times, however, I see leaders struggling to make an impact because:

---

[1] https://www.forbes.com/sites/mikemyatt/2013/10/10/a-crisis-of-leadership-whats-next/#781261965000

- some don't know how to be leaders, and organisations are not doing a good job of helping them to become leaders (it doesn't happen overnight, even if one is purposed);
- some people attained leadership positions because they were great individual contributors, but as leaders they are required to motivate and drive the performance of a team, and that's not really what they signed up for—but no one turns down a promotion;
- some are leaders simply because they wanted the title and money, and once they have them, it's unlikely they can or will inspire others to follow them.

The goal of this book is to help you understand that you are purposed for leadership and then to encourage you to step up and out, into that call. That will require you to put in the effort and sacrifice to become a leader who *inspires*, *serves*, and *connects* with those you lead and who willingly follow you so that together you can no longer remain invisible if you have been invisible up to this point.

WHAT DOES IT MEAN TO INSPIRE OTHERS?

I have come to realise I cannot motivate another person because their true motivation is intrinsic, which varies from person to person. I can, however, inspire and help them draw on their inner drive to achieve and excel. I can become the kind of leader who inspires others by:

- *Being a good communicator*—learning the art of active listening and presence.
- *Being an independent thinker*—pushing the envelope; willing to challenge the status quo; and inviting others to challenge, and question ideas (even mine), as well as acting courageously.
- *Showing up with passion*—bringing energy;

daring to stand up for my convictions and values; refusing to use a manipulative method; valuing substance over form, not quitting on important things, and speaking truth to power; and relentlessly pursuing the goal, even though to achieve it will also risk failure along the way.
- *Envisioning the possibilities*—painting a vivid picture of the future for others to see, daring them to dream and dream big; and, 'putting feet to that vision.'

WHAT DOES IT MEAN TO SERVE OTHERS?

You may have heard or read about the concept of servant leadership to which I alluded above. In essence, it's leaders putting other's interests first (the last shall be first) ahead of their own. As a leader, you make serving relevant by:

- *Caring for others*—being truly concerned for the well-being of others, providing support, encouragement, and accountability, sometimes through tough love;
- *Helping others succeed*—putting the success of others before your own by drawing out and developing their greatness, then being excited for their victories;
- *Forgiveness*—being able to put aside perceived wrongs and differences to help the person, letting go of anger quickly, and not allowing resentment to build;
- *Humility*—putting ego aside, not needing to be right and not needing to be the centre of attention or the one who gets the accolades, while giving praise to another when praise is due;
- *Trustworthiness*—being a person of integrity

by meaning what you say and saying it honestly, doing to others what you would have them do to you, and operating from right motives (using things not people).

WHAT DOES IT TAKE TO CONNECT WITH OTHERS?

Connecting with others is much more than good communication. It means you being you, and that requires:

- *Being authentic*—being who you are and not who you assume you ought to be, and being vulnerable as you exercise good judgement; this is an important part of overcoming invisibility;
- *Accepting Others*—giving people the same right as you have to be who they are and to shed the expectations of who they are not. This acceptance is not based on race, religion, colour, gender, or sexual orientation, but rather on the things that make a person unique: their passions, personality, purpose, and principles, which is everything that shapes how they see their world;
- *Likeability*—this is not about charisma but emanates from character. The good news is character can be developed if one has the heart and motivation to learn. Leaders are likeable when they're optimistic, reliable, and attentive to their team's purpose and aspirations, and also when they balance work and fun. They know how to collaborate, to ensure the whole team is engaged, and to make certain that the rules of engagement are fair and they smile—a lot!

I am a five-feet two inch black woman, and recently turned fifty as I write. I have often been overlooked as a leader, even though I exhibited leadership traits at an early age. I know all too well what it is like to feel "invisible." As a teenager, I didn't fit in but had little idea as to the reason why, and as an adult, I often felt misunderstood. Even though I'm not the shy, retiring type, I did not go to the best schools, was not the most talented child in my primary or university classes, and did not have any other environmental or circumstantial privileges leaders are perceived to have. I was and still am an independent thinker prone to "telling it like it is," with a gift for envisioning all the possibilities in a situation. This meant I rarely accepted the status quo or conformed. If only I had understood my unique personality and purpose before I reached the age of 40—but it's never too late.

You may identify with not fitting in or the equally painful experience of working hard to fit in but still feeling like an outsider—like you are invisible. Like me, perhaps you have been (or are) frustrated as deep down you know you are a leader, but have not had the recognition up to this point. Maybe you have taken the safe road and not spoken up, content with playing a lesser role or making yourself invisible so that others would not reject you or to protect yourself. This book will encourage you not to give up and equip you to step up to the fullness of your potential, and then to step out to serve and lead. Leadership is not a destination but a journey. It is not about the title you hold but rather the impact you make in the lives of those you serve; people like your family, work colleagues, customers, and ministry team.

Have you ever been in a meeting or other group setting where you were not the formal leader but found people listen to you? Just by being there, things shift and you make things happen. Or where you know you have some nugget of wisdom and it's the very thing needed to address the road block or progress the project, if people would just give you a chance, or grasp what you are saying? You felt unheard or misunderstood—in effect, invisible. At times like those, you may have wondered if you were off base or if you had a totally wrong perspective. You go back and re-group, however, only to find weeks or even years later that you were on point but no one could see it at the time. They were not ready for it, and perhaps neither were you (more on that later).

So come with me as I share my personal journey from being an invisible leader to accepting my role as a visible leader, executive coach, and consultant to governments and corporations. My hope is that this book will be a call to action if you are purposed for leadership but have not accepted the call. If you are already a leader, I hope to challenge you to ask "Why am I a leader?" I also want to encourage you to develop the character needed for authentic leadership that will enable you to successfully emerge from the shadows of being an invisible leader to a visible one. Let's begin the journey now.

Felicia Linch
October 2019

CHAPTER 1
LEADERS DON'T FAIL: LEARNING TO FAIL FORWARD

*"Success is not final, failure is not fatal:
it is the courage to continue that counts."*
- Winston Churchill

I was standing there, studying the board where the results of my law bar finals, the exams I had to pass to become a U.K. barrister, had finally been posted. I remembered the past trepidation and fear I had when I went to discover the results for my university law degree. Those same fears swept over me again. This time, the list was long, but then I realised the painful truth: My name was not on the passed list.

I checked again and then allowed my gaze to look at the fail list just below the passes. This list was also long, but that is where I found my name. I had failed. I was so upset I couldn't speak or even cry; I could barely breathe. Things had not been going well in my life, but I was a hard-working student and no one, including myself, expected me to fail. I wasn't going to be top of the class, but for sure I would have done more than enough to pass. There were so many students at the board looking with me, and I knew many of them, but I didn't hear or see a thing. I was in my own world, trying to process the truth: I had failed.

I had never failed at anything in my life, but that's not to say my life was without adversity. My parents separated and later divorced when I was about six years old. My mum gave up her custody battle to my dad since he was determined to fight for it, and the scenario got ugly with social workers and others intervening. After that, my outlook on life changed. I was a child one might describe as having a sunny disposition, but that also changed. Instead of expecting the best, whenever life was going well, I started expecting fate to step in with adversity.

As a young woman, I had suffered bouts of depression, yet always felt that was not who I was supposed to be: a depressed person. After all, my English name, Felicia, means happy. I knew happy was who I was, but somehow the real me struggled to come out. I learned to overcome the adversity and the depression by doing two things. The first was journaling, which allowed me to process all my thoughts, however bizarre, without being judged.

The second was by being busy and focused. At an early age and with Mum no longer living in the house, I assumed much responsibility for the running of the household, not because I had to, but because I felt it was my responsibility, especially since I had a little sister, Chi. That gave me a reason to always get up and keep pushing on. You might ask, "Since you had been through adversity in your life before, why was this failure such a big deal?" It was a big deal because my life plan was hinged on this one event: passing the bar.

After university, I moved back home, the consequences of which I knew were going to be complicated. I had matured and grown by then and wanted to spread my wings. My dad's rules, which in retrospect were not terribly restrictive, proved to be a problem after I had enjoyed the independence of living on my own. What's more, I had a boyfriend who was eight years older than I. My lifestyle choices eventually led to my leaving home and moving into a shared flat with strangers. After this, my dad and I, who had always been close, ended up barely speaking.

After I moved out, I was financially on my own. I give my dad credit, for he said no matter what, he would pay my tuition and fees, which he saw as his responsibility as my father. That was gracious; many parents would have cut off funds when their child rebelled or sought to be independent. Even so, I had to take a full-time job, working mostly nights, and went to bar school during the day. Life became even more complicated because my boyfriend was separated from his wife when I met him, but she eventually returned.

He was born in India, was brought to the U.K. when young, but was Westernised in all his ways. He had an arranged marriage with a woman born and raised in India and after a few years, it wasn't working out for either of them, so she returned to India. His brother told me, "I know you make him happy, but you know this is going nowhere. He can't be with a black girl." After the family had persuaded the wife to come back with a daughter I had not known about, I was caught up in an affair with this married man.

There I was, working at Pizza Hut to earn a living while in a complicated relationship, and I'd failed the bar exams. What had kept me from going crazy in the midst of all that adversity was I had a focused goal. After I completed university in Cardiff, Wales, I wanted to go back there to live. I had secured a pupillage, which is a mandatory apprenticeship one has to do in the U.K. to qualify as a barrister. I had even found a flat and paid a deposit. In the moment when I found my name on the failed list, that future, along with achieving my goal, both vanished. Pupillage was conditional on passing my bar finals.

The more I tried to process my results, the more I couldn't get a handle on it. I had yet to learn that "failure isn't fatal." On that day, it felt like it was. I took the Tube home, curled up in bed and didn't eat for the rest of the day; a big thing for a foodie like me. Morning came and I neither ate nor showered. Depression was setting in, only this time I had nothing to focus on, no goal to keep me going. Unlike my past adversity, which had always been due to external circumstances, messing up my life was all down to me. I had no plan B. People in the Okosi family (my maiden name) didn't have a plan B.

The year before university, I had to apply to the clearinghouse system. My college tutor had advised everyone to also apply for polytechnics, which at the time were the lower-grade Institutions. I told my dad about that and he replied, "Why would you apply there? You're going to university," and he promptly tore up the polytechnic application. To this day, I still don't employ a plan B if I've set my sights on a goal. I find having a way out of my goal dilutes my conviction rather than helping me to focus as I push towards achieving the goal.

Lying in bed and depressed, I tried to process what it all meant. How could this have happened? In fact, how could any of it have happened? How could I have gotten so far away from my values that I was seeing a married man, living with strangers, and then failing in the career I'd spent my life being groomed for? Eventually my flat mate, Sarah the landlady's daughter, came in to say, "Come on, Babe. You've got to get up, you know you can. You're going to beat this."

All I could think is, "This cosseted little rich girl has no clue." She had a car while at university and maintained quite the lifestyle—or so I thought. Moreover, she had recently "found God" and was annoyingly upbeat about life, including my problems. She would often encourage me and say, "Babe, I know you believe in God, you're so close. You just need to change your lifestyle." Little did Sarah or I know how far from the truth that was. We both came to realise that behaviour change is seldom sustainable, but personal transformation, the kind that comes from the heart, holds the key to life and peace—and that requires much more.

Even though I was devastated, I was grateful for the encouragement. Sarah wasn't the only encouraging voice I had. I had always been close to my two siblings: my brother and Chi, my sister—we were kind of like the Three Musketeers. Far from being ashamed to tell them what was happening with me, I told them all of it and was relieved. As always, they gave me nothing but love and support, with no judgment. We all need people like that in our lives, whether friends or family.

ADDING INSULT TO INJURY

A week after the results, a friend from bar school called. She had also failed and was angrily shouting on the phone, "Did you see all those who failed were black or ethnic, every one of them?" At first I could not take in what she was implying since I had experienced racism only a few times as a young adult. Once, when my brother and I were with some of his friends in his friend's dad's Mercedes, we got pulled over by the police. The pretext for the stop was, "We thought you had a broken tail light. On seeing it wasn't broken they said, "We'll just do some checks anyway." They thought the car was stolen. Therefore, I couldn't identify with my friends and peers who had experienced racism in a more significant way.

After the call from my friend, I walked to the pass/fail board again and it felt like another punch in the stomach. I couldn't deny that all the names on the failed list were unpronounceable and like me, were ethnic. "Can it really be that? Surely not, for this is the starting point of the British establishment." I decided I would leave it right there, but several others also thought there was a race element involved in the results. The Black Lawyers Association called a meeting with students who had failed expressing their disgust and promising to support them in taking action. I went to the meeting but was still incredulous that it really could be an issue of racism. It was not until I had my feedback session at bar school that reality finally hit me.

I had failed two courses. One was advocacy, which was my strongest subject, and negotiation skills, a close second. It was made more painful by the fact that I had failed each exam by one mark—one lousy mark. I knew in the advocacy I had gotten a point of law wrong and I even told the assessor so directly after I finished. I was reassured that it wouldn't matter much because the key skills test was on advocacy, which is presenting a case.

The exams were video recorded and my assessor, an accomplished barrister, advised that we watch it together first and then he would give me feedback. I watched it and cringed at the technical mistake in the advocacy exam, but still I felt overall it wasn't that bad. After both videos had played, my assessor said, "Well, I looked at this a few times because I couldn't see what you had done wrong. Sure you made a small error on the law, but it was clear you knew you had. Really, there's not much to say. Take the re-sit and you'll definitely get it next time," he advised.

As I left the room, tears streamed down my face. I finally believed it possible that I had been the victim of racism. It was all too much for me to process and back I went to curl up in my bed and hope when I came up for air it would all be over like a bad dream—which wasn't the case. My friend called, asking if I had given thought to the meeting with the Black Lawyers Association. I had and was faced with one of the hardest decisions I have ever had to make. I'm accustomed to standing up for rights; after all, isn't that what being a lawyer is all about? Yet I wasn't sure what I wanted to achieve or what was possible to achieve by protesting the results.

I spoke with my dad because I was in desperate need of help and counsel. He asked what outcome I wanted in this situation? I replied I wanted to qualify. He suggested I think through the options offering the best chance of qualifying. I knew right then if I wanted to qualify, I had to be invisible and keep quiet. It was a bitter pill to swallow because I had chosen to study law in part because I was idealistic. I had discovered I cared deeply about justice issues and my failure was not justice. I recognised even then, however, that if I wanted to change the system, I had to be on the inside. I could not bring change from the outside looking in, therefore, I swallowed my pride, kept quiet, and re-sat the exam.

LETTING GO

In 1992, after I passed my re-sit for the bar finals, I decided to take a much needed break while I tried to find a pupillage. I continued to work full-time at Pizza Hut where I had become a senior supervisor, managing shifts and training new recruits. Ash and I were still together, but his wife had returned by this time. He said he still wanted out of that relationship and since we'd already been together for 18 months by the time she returned, I believed him. Time moved on and somehow his getting out wasn't happening.

Eventually, after we'd been away on holiday, his wife got hold of my home number and called me. We spoke and the absurd thing was she seemed pleasant, as much as one could be in those circumstances, even understanding how the relationship could have happened. She let me know I was not the first one. Then she said she had found a picture and described it. I knew the photo which was taken at Pizza Hut with my work team. She asked, "Are you the Italian one? The last one was Italian."

I replied, "No, I'm the black lady on the other side."

At that point, she screamed, "How could he? You're, you're *black*?"

My sadness over this awkward situation was quickly replaced with anger. Fortunately, she hung up before I could give her a piece of my mind. After the call, I sat on the stairs reflecting, *She can't help it. They're Hindus and have a caste system and being black is equated with the lowest caste.* Just as I had calmed down, she called back and asked. "Are you free today? Will you come to the house to meet me? I don't drive."

For some reason, I felt compelled to say yes. I made my way to the house, even though I wasn't driving either. I sat on the bus reflecting on how I'd gotten into this mess. Ash was at work and we talked. At the end, I resolved that if she wanted to try and make a go of her marriage, I would not get in the way. I made a promise that day not to see Ash again. He then returned home and was obviously shocked to see me in his living room. We informed him of our decision and I left.

Ash tried to call me, but I ignored him, determined to keep my promise. I moved house and changed jobs. I went to work for a bailiff's company close to my new home—ten minutes from home if I walked. It was a horrible job because I was responsible for taking calls from people who owed debts to the local council government and then making arrangements with them to pay off the debt. It was stressful calling people who had no money to ask them to pay bills or else bailiff's would come and take all their belongings. Christmas in a bailiff's company was especially heart-breaking., for we would ruthlessly seize toys, gifts, and anything that wasn't nailed down or deemed necessary for the purposes of earning a living to satisfy someone's debt. I often found myself trying to make payment arrangements that were not in compliance with company policy.

Maybe it was the stress of the previous two years, but one day I was coming home from the supermarket and I literally collapsed in the street. I was burned out, mentally and physically. Thankfully, I didn't live too far and passers-by made sure I got home safely. What followed was months of tests trying to determine if it was Chronic Fatigue Syndrome, Fibromyalgia, or a reoccurrence of Glandular Fever (Mono). They didn't know what it was. I was pumped full of antibiotics and was getting worse. I did recover but it took a few months and my health was never the same. To this day, when my life gets out of balance and I am striving rather than flowing with peace, the same symptoms reoccur.

My confidence had taken a severe beating since failing my bar finals. Once a confident woman who loved to speak in public and be on camera, I had become withdrawn. I was more than a little lost, and I felt like I no longer knew who I was. I had often quoted Nietzche's line, *"That which does not kill us only makes us stronger,"* but I didn't believe that any longer. I knew I had to get on with my career at the bar, and my life needed meaning.

I decided to leave my job at the bailiff's company which gave me lots of time to reflect. I decided it was time to go back to law. I got a job in local government that was legally-related and would help my attempt to obtain another pupillage, this time in London. I moved into a flat, with a woman named Sue, located in my old stomping grounds of South London.

I was admitted to the bar in 1994. My admittance ceremony should have been a celebration, but it was far from that. My mum came to the ceremony and was as supportive as ever, but my dad did not. We were not on speaking terms when I went to see him less than a week before my admittance. I summoned the courage to invite him, but I wasn't sure he would come, especially given the way I had left home while attending bar school. After the ceremony, I asked him why he hadn't come, and he said, "I went to Temple Station and couldn't find it. If you had given me proper instructions and adequate warning, I would not have gotten lost. In the end, I gave up and came home."

My dad never gives up. He was still angry with me,

so much so that he wasn't there to celebrate the thing he too had worked so hard to see come to pass, for bar school was not cheap. More than that, he'd been grooming me for this all my life. His not being there felt like a bride getting married and her father not being present on her wedding day. Around then, I started to journal again, which always helped me process things.

Whilst work kept me busy, I had also found another way to deal with adverse situations and that was to take myself out of them. I found a new activity to focus on, and that was exercise. I eventually realised that exercise was not enough to shake my feelings of failure as a daughter. I had to get rid of the negative self-talk in my head if I was going to move on. I started to read self-help books and learn about the power of positive declarations. I made a deliberate effort to watch my speech and not to entertain the negativity of others. I'm an optimistic person by nature but depression has a way of keeping one in a box. I decided enough was enough.

FAILING FORWARD IS A LEARNING EXPERIENCE FOR EVERYONE.

This chapter speaks to failure and disappointment and how to handle them. It's one of the more important lessons we learn as leaders—that failure need not be final or fatal. Once we become leaders, it opens the door for more chances to fail. In fact, as a leader we may fail publicly because we are out front and can't play it safe or sit on the sidelines any longer. The key is to accept that we will fail, grieve it if we must, learn from it, and then get up and keep going. In other words, fail forward because we have a purpose to fulfil and people to serve. Failing and moving forward can inspire those we serve, if they see it, and, we allow them access to it by discussing and learning from it. Our failure also gives them permision to do the same.

Many people fear failure which is the reason some people prefer to remain invisible. By doing so, they protect themselves from failure, but also prevent themselves from ever stepping up and out to become the leaders they were purposed to be.

CHAPTER 2
TURNING THE CORNER: FINDING THE COURAGE TO CHANGE

*"Courage starts with showing up and
letting ourselves be seen."*
- Brene' Brown, author of *Daring Greatly*

In 1996, I finally secured a pupillage in a chambers known for defence work. Four years after failing my bar finals. I had a new boyfriend, Michael, who was single, a business owner, and quite generous. I was having fun with him and my pupillage was icing on the cake.

I recall my first day of pupillage. I went to court with Bob, the head of chambers and a somewhat odd fellow. I didn't know the reason why he was odd at the time, but given the work I do now, I realize he was definitely lacking in emotional intelligence. We were getting ready to go to court, and I was in his office while he briefed me on a case. He then proceeded to take off his jumper. I thought nothing of it until then his shirt came off and he was standing there bare-chested and hairy.

He proceeded to robe up for court and all the while kept talking as if nothing untoward had just occurred. We went to court and arrived back in chambers at Bob's office. He began a debrief, asking me questions to see what I had observed. All of a sudden, he dived beneath his desk, I presumed into his briefcase since I couldn't see, all the while still talking from below the desk. When he finally came up for air, he said, "I think I've left my pen."

"Pen?" I said bemused.

He said, "Yes, my pen. In the courtroom. You need to go back and get it."

By then, my hackles were up as I had heard stories about how pupils were treated in some chambers like errand boys and girls. I had struggled long and hard to get where I was and I was there to learn. It was my first day so I sat still and just listened.

He continued, "Yes, I remember now, I must have dropped it. You'll likely have to look on the floor," he explained.

At this point, I couldn't contain myself and said, "Do I look like I came dressed to crawl on the floor looking for your pen?" I was dressed in my suit and heels. Before the poor man could say anything, I got up and said, "This time I'll do it, but this is the last time!" I went to the courtroom and retrieved his pen. Bob never asked me to do anything like that again. In that situation, I had refused to be invisible!

My pupillage lasted twelve months. During the first six months, the pupil shadows the pupil master and during the second six months, the pupils are "on their feet"—let loose to take cases of their own, mainly small matters. My pupil master, who was a mistress, was named Tessa and was quite the star. She was of Jewish background who was not only bright but also stylish and fun—when she wasn't shouting. Tessa had two pupils. I was one and the other was a young woman named Ali. When Tessa came to work in a bad mood, we would sit like school children in silence so we would not irritate her. One day, however, Tessa went too far. She asked me to go and ask the clerks about one of her cases. I duly went and when I returned with the bad news, she said, "What the f___?" and proceeded to throw a book at me.

I calmly picked up the book and started to pack my bag. She asked, "Where are you going?" to which I replied, "Home, and when you can learn to behave like an adult, I'll come back," and I left.

The next morning I got a call from chambers asking me to come in since Tessa had left something for me. I arrived in the clerks' room and was given a present. I walked back to Tessa's room and she said, "Hi, about yesterday, sorry."

I said, "It's fine. Let's just not let it happen again."

I had wanted to practice housing law like Tessa. It was a good fit with the work I had done in local government and was a real opportunity to help vulnerable people. I was also delivering workshops for Shelter, a homeless charity. My love and skill for advocacy, however, was returning. I was being asked to handle more and more hearings for the criminal lawyers in chambers.

I was in the magistrates court defending a taxi driver for soliciting a fare where he should not have. Another taxi driver there on the same charge was so impressed by the fact that my client was acquitted that he told his solicitor he wanted me to represent him. His solicitor was a lovely woman called Cissy who was a breath of fresh air. Most solicitors knew that the power in the legal profession was skewed towards them because barristers don't have direct client contact in the U.K. A client contacts a solicitor and then they instruct barristers. Even though barristers are often seen as the more glamorous or prestigious side of the profession, the solicitors have the power to decide if the barrister works or not. That makes many of them cocky or flat out arrogant. Worse, if the barrister is female, some suggest they need to "ingratiate" one's self with them to succeed.

Cissy was different. She was pleasant to deal with and not puffed up like so many of the others, especially those from her firm. It seems her client saw something in me and she encouraged me at a time when I had begun yet again to second-guess myself. I had applied for a civil tenancy (a full-time position) in the area of housing law, but I didn't get it. I began to torture myself with negative self-talk like, "Can I really do this?" At the same time, I was doing well in crime, getting more important and complex cases, and I was reconsidering whether being a criminal lawyer would be such a bad thing after all.

Cissy's firm had quite the reputation in chambers. Most of the criminal barristers were climbing over themselves to get work from them. They had an annual Christmas party, a grand affair, to which only "special" people were invited. Amazingly, I got an invite. To say that elevated me within chambers was an understatement. Pupils were beginning to compete viciously for tenancies and I just racked up critical points, which were much needed. After that, I got placed with one of the rising stars on the criminal side whose name was Andy. He saw something in me and took me under his wing. He started to give me his hearings while he attended to more pressing matters.

On one occasion, I had to take the arraignment of a man who had been charged with grievous bodily harm (GBH) on an 18-month-old baby, having beaten her to within an inch of her life. When I viewed the evidence the night before, I began to weep. There was no baby in the photos, just a red blob, and it was a miracle she survived. I sat in the cell opposite this man and tried to understand how he could be trying to enter a plea of not guilty. The more I spoke to him, the more convinced I became that he needed to enter a plea of insanity, but that was not going to happen. I finally asked to see the judge. I had reached the point where I needed to say, "I am asking to be released."

He asked, "Are you professionally embarrassed" That means there is some reason, other than the nature of the case, such as lacking sufficient experience or competence to handle the matter. It can also indicate that circumstances arose to make it difficult to maintain professional independence or the administration of justice might be prejudiced.

I replied, "No, I just don't think I would be the best person to represent this man, for as far as I'm concerned, a not-guilty plea is absurd and I don't think it's in his best interests."

The judge said, "If you're not professionally embarrassed, I could insist you go ahead. Are you sure you're not professionally embarrassed? Perhaps you're too junior and lack the experience in this matter being a pupil?"

I replied, "Yes, perhaps so".

He said, "You're released."

As I turned to walk out the door, he said, "For what it's worth, I think you would have done just fine."

As I sat on the train that day, I began to question, after all the struggle and effort to get where I was, whether the bar was really for me. I had a conversation a few weeks earlier with a senior member of chambers while representing a minor in the juvenile court. It was the second time I had represented the same youth and had given him a good talking to, like he was my own. I told the senior, "It's heartbreaking to watch these youngsters. I feel like we're putting a band-aid on things, but we're not getting to the heart of the matter."

He smiled and replied, "Don't knock it, seeing how you've already represented him twice." He continued, "That's how you build your career. As they grow on to 'bigger and better things.' you'll go with them. They're your future meal ticket."

I was speechless, for that was not the reason I had come to the bar. I wanted to see young people like this young man avoid a life of crime. That was not what justice was about. I got back to chambers and met with Andy, the rising star to whom I had been assigned. He had heard what happened, for the bar is a small world. I asked him, "How do you deal with cases like that?"

He responded, "Everyone deserves a fair trial."

I said, "That's a cop out. That's law school ideology and not the real world. You're about to be a father, how does it make you feel?"

He said, "We do our job." Then and there I knew I didn't have much longer at the bar. This was not for me.

WHAT NOW?

Not long before I left chambers, Cissy invited me to her wedding. She was a Christian, and she had spoken to me about her faith on several occasions. Whilst I still had a belief in God, I had decided some time earlier that Christianity was not for me. I was more "spiritual" and believed that all roads led home to God, no matter what faith one chose to practice. Nonetheless, I accepted her invite since I wanted to celebrate with her. Besides, I loved weddings and still do.

I had not been to church for a long time, and certainly not one like hers. The wedding was not in a grand old church building but in a modern, pre-fabricated building in Hackney. There was much excitement and a lot of gospel singing. It was a real celebration with lots of people dressed in vibrant colours. I grew up in the Catholic church and it was nothing like that. Cissy looked amazing and positively radiant. I imagined that was how I would like to look on my wedding day.

I was there with my partner, Michael, whom I no longer called my boyfriend. I was too grown up for that. As I listened to the sermon, I felt a huge wave of sadness engulf me, as if I felt the weight of all my mistakes and things I knew were not right in my life at that moment. Next thing I knew, I was crying, not small sniffles, but loud sobs with large tears. I had no idea why this was happening, especially at a wedding. I made my way to the back of the large auditorium, and as I sat there still sobbing, I felt a presence like never before. I wasn't at all sure what it was, but slowly but surely I felt calm, and for the first time in a long time, I felt hope. In that moment, my heart changed. How it changed or what transpired, I didn't know. *Could this be the "Jesus thing" Cissy and Sarah, my former landlady's daughter, had spoken to me about?*

I knew that day was the start of something different, but I didn't know what it was. I had been learning from my past mistakes and failures, and had managed to keep moving forward, striving to achieve my goal to become a barrister. Yet I knew there was a void in my life. The strange thing is that I had not recognised it until then because things were clearly improving.

As the wedding ceremony closed, I had regained my composure. I felt lighter. Michael met me at the back and inquired, "You okay?"

I said, "Yes, better than okay."

COURAGE INSPIRES PEOPLE

This chapter describes finding the courage to make a change, and not letting the past determine your future. As leaders, recognising when it's time to move on is critical. It's one of the things Seth Godin speaks about in his book The Dip—knowing when to quit. Quitting takes courage because people may see us as a failure. They may be disappointed because we didn't meet their expectations. We must know when it's time to move on and then have the courage to do so. Courage inspires people and that's key to becoming a visible leader because as the opening quote says—it requires showing up and letting ourselves be seen.

CHAPTER 3
PURPOSED FOR LEADERSHIP: THE JOURNEY TO SELF-AWARENESS

"Self-awareness is difficult to measure because we are innately wired for self-deception."

- Jenni Catron, *The Four Dimensions of Extraordinary Leadership: The Power of Leading from Your Heart, Soul, Mind and Strength*

After Cissy's wedding, there was a spiritual shift in my life. Don't get me wrong. It's not like one of those religious scenes where I fell to the floor, confessed my sins, and experienced a radical transformation. It was more of a gradual change that took place on the inside of me. I had always had a sense of someone, perhaps God, being present in my life, but I had not understood who Jesus was. For me, Jesus was a story or a concept, but not a real person—all that began to change.

In my younger days, I had an intense interest in faith. At age ten, I went with my Saturday cookery teacher from our Catholic girl's group to see the Pope. We waited for hours in a huge crowd, excited to glimpse just the top of his head, but thankfully there were big screens on which to see it all. As I grew older, the church seemed unable to speak to the challenges I faced in life. It all seemed irrelevant. After the wedding, that feeling of God's presence returned. It's hard to describe what that presence felt like, but it was coupled with a sense of destiny. What does that mean? For me, it was recognising my life was no accident, but was significant and worth protecting because God had protected me on numerous occasions.

I was a tomboy when I was young and loved climbing, despite being told on too many occasions that was not the way I should conduct myself, especially as a girl. When I was about eight years old and was playing outside with friends, an incident happened, and I sensed God was right there with me. We were playing tag and I was determined to win. They cornered me on the first-floor balcony of my mum's flat in Manchester, and I decided the only way to escape was to go over the balcony. It wasn't one of my smartest decisions.

As I scrambled to get over the balcony, I lost my footing and fell backwards. I landed hard on the sleeping policeman below and after the children stopped screaming, there was silence. (A sleeping policeman is one of those concrete pillars erected as a barricade to prevent cars from going through.) I just lay strewn over this pillar, wondering if I was going to be paralysed and certain I must have broken my back. I was thinking, *God, I know that wasn't smart, but please . . .* As I tried rolling over, I noticed how I felt no pain. I thought it meant I had lost my ability to feel. As I stood up and checked myself, I realised I was perfectly fine, without a scratch, and

I have never to this day suffered from back pain as a result of that incident.

At age twelve, I was cooking, something not uncommon in African households, since children often learn to cook at an early age. In those days, we had eye-level grills and we also had curtains in the kitchen. I was preparing chips (or fries as they call them in the U.S. and other places) when the pan went up in flames. I watched as the curtains caught fire, spreading all along the kitchen. I remember calling out to God, as many of us do in a crisis, "God, please don't let us die. I know I'm not doing quite what I should, but please!" Immediately, the fire went out, like someone had blown out a candle. My brother and I just looked at each other in disbelief, but thoroughly relieved. We took down the curtains and put up new ones so my dad never knew what happened.

By the time I was seventeen, I had discovered a social conscience, realising that justice was important to me. I was working on a paper for my A-Level social studies exam on the topic of the institutionalisation of young black men. As I was leaving a mental health facility I had been visiting in Tulse Hill, not far from Brixton, I was intent on not missing my bus. I ran across the road and didn't see the speeding car. The car hit me and my body went flying through the air. I landed hard on the ground and heard screeching of brakes as a car stopped near the top of my head.

As I lay there, I could hear the driver say he thought I was dead. The funniest thing was all I could think was, "Do I have on decent underwear?" I heard my mother's voice warning me about wearing clean, decent underwear in case I was ever in an accident (Mum was a nurse). I got up and once again was grateful to find I didn't have a scratch on me. God's presence was there yet again.

Seeing no scratches, I simply wanted to get on the bus and go home, but the driver and passers-by insisted I go to the hospital. I didn't want the fuss. I knew my dad, like any parent, would be panicking when he heard his daughter was in the hospital, not to mention my mum who would have to be told by phone since we lived in London and she was in Manchester. I did go to the hospital and my dad did run in panicking wondering what had happened. All I could say was, "I was running for the bus."

I couldn't deny that God was protecting me and it had to be for a reason. I thought bar school was it so I could become a defender of justice, but that wasn't it. That meant I had yet to discover what the "it" was.

LEAVING THE LAW

When I decided the bar wasn't for me, it didn't mean law wasn't. I was as passionate as ever about justice for people and there was an alternative. I decided to do the Qualified Lawyers Transfer Test (QLLTT) and become a solicitor. It meant more exams but at least I didn't have to go back to full-time education, which I couldn't afford. Contrary to popular opinion, people don't make much money at the bar. They usually have to wait months, sometimes years, to get paid if they are doing legal aid work, where the state pays the client's fees. Therefore, most Barristers live on debt. Chambers print out your aged-debt report which you take to your bank. The bank then gives you a loan based on how much you are owed. I knew I needed proper paid work and being a solicitor would fit that bill.

I completed the QLLTT and became a solicitor. I moved to a successful local firm and was able to purchase a two-bedroom flat right next to Wandsworth Common, a nice, safe area with lovely shops and restaurants. Life was looking up, but the business wasn't doing well. It was a small legal aid practice and I had become more involved in the business side, not just the client side. We were a small, close-knit team and we eventually came to the conclusion that something drastic needed to be done. My choices were to buy in as an equity partner or leave. I chose to leave.

I had two good offers and chose to go to a larger firm in Camden, which offered me significantly more money once they knew I had another offer. I was a good negotiator for other people but not for myself, for I didn't believe I was worth it. At my new firm, I became more and more involved in the business side and in particular HR and training, and I loved it. I was given more responsibility and was being groomed for partnership. My head of department was a bright young woman, but her leadership skills needed refinement. She would frequently lose her temper with staff and the whole office dreaded working with her.

One day, she had let rip at me again because one of her cases I had been handling in her absence wasn't progressing as she expected. She didn't ask why, but instead started bawling me out in our open plan office. I sat there until she was finished and then, as she always did, she went about her business like nothing had happened. Later after I calmed down, I cornered her in the stationary cupboard. I shut the door so it was just the two of us and said, "Did you ever think to ask why it was not progressing as expected?"

She said ,"No, but . . ." I cut her off to explain why.

I continued, "Anyway, I don't care about that. When are you going to learn that it's not okay to behave like that? You come in here every day, bawl people out, embarrassing and intimidating them. Even if you have a reason, you shouldn't speak to people like that. For sure, this is the last time you will speak to me in that manner. Do you hear me?"

She was stunned. No one had ever spoken to her like that, but I had decided enough was enough. I could no longer be invisible when she acted like that. I had to step up to confront her and step out to speak the truth. She asked if we could go for a drink and I agreed. We became good friends after that, but as the department grew, it became clear that while she was an amazing lawyer and individual contributor, she was a hopelessly-poor manager, as were many of the partners.

The time for annual performance appraisals came. Mine went well with no surprises, even though I hadn't quite made my targets, I was doing many other things in the firm. My boss and friend said at the end of the appraisal, "So, we're done?"

I said, "Not quite," and stepped up and out one more time. I proceeded to give her feedback that day as a manager and addressed where she needed some further help or training, I knew nothing about coaching in those days. Before I had finished, she burst into tears. I sat with her and explained, "I'm not being mean; I want you to get better".

She said, "I know, and I've been struggling."

After that discussion, the senior partner spoke with me: "We owe you. We've let this slide for far too long but we didn't know how to tell her."

At that point, I asked myself, "Who's managing who?" More than that, I realised I could influence others, not manipulate them, and enjoyed leading and especially helping our team. I had not noticed that till then, and the more leadership and management work I undertook, the more my passion and confidence came back, but it wasn't for the law. I had been invisible where my love and skills for management and leadership were concerned. It was time for me to step out.

I went home and researched management programmes and discovered a programme called an MBA. Not long after, I decided to re-mortgage my house, go back to full-time study, and complete an MBA. Law wasn't for me after all, but I was still passionate about justice and wondered how all that would fit together. I decided I didn't know, but I was determined to find out.

DISCOVERING HIM

Just before I left university, I was wrestling with my career choices. My path was set to become a lawyer, and as far as my dad was concerned, my next stop was to become a judge. Even then, however, I had started to get into business books and was loving it. I thought briefly about shifting gears and pursuing a business degree. I realise now that purpose is always knocking if we are willing to listen and respond. Fear and expectation stopped me from thinking about it more, but I recall having quite a few sleepless nights. In a sense, I chose to be invisible where my interest for business was concerned and cloaked myself in a lawyer's garb.

One night in particular I was "awakened." I use that word deliberately because it felt like someone was waking me but there was no one there. I sensed a presence, which wasn't frightening; in fact, it was quite calming. I got up and tried to avoid looking in the mirror. (From an early age, I disliked mirrors since I expected to see someone in them other than me—I'm not a fan of horror movies.) This time though, it was like the presence was saying, "I'm the one you've been avoiding in the mirror." I recognised at that time it was Jesus, and the presence was distinct and palpable.

I moved from the bed and decided to 'front it out.' I stood in front of the mirror and opened my eyes, but there was nothing. At that point, I said calmly but boldly, "I don't want to see you. Whatever plans you may have for me, I have my own plans, so leave me alone." The restless nights did not return and I seldom felt that presence again—until later in my life.

Around the time I left law and started my MBA, much was happening. I had re-gained my faith and was attending an evangelical church. It was quite different from my Catholic upbringing, not just in-terms of style, but in the way people like my friend Cissy spoke about Jesus. When I grew up in the Catholic church, I knew who Jesus was, or at least the theology of who He was: Son of God, died on the cross, and redeemed mankind through that sacrifice. All of it had been more like concepts and not living truths. What I discovered over the ensuing months was that Jesus was a real person and I didn't know Him. In fact, I realised I had actually rejected wanting to know Him.

In my final month before leaving my law firm, I decided to get baptised. It was a great celebration, especially since my sister and I were getting baptised together. Easter was a few weeks away and Cissy asked me to join her on a women's retreat. I thought, *I'm not sure I'm ready for that.* She kept asking me and the more she did, the more resolute I became about not going. Two days before the retreat, I couldn't sleep. I opened my eyes and the first thing I thought about was the retreat. I groaned because I knew I was supposed to go. I muttered out loud, "Alright, *now* can I get some sleep?" and I did. I went straight to sleep.

The retreat was intense. We arose at 6 AM for prayers, attended praise and worship services, had sessions all day, then more prayers, and evening praise and worship from 8 PM to 9 PM. I am *not* an early bird, and cannot say I awakened with the "joy of the Lord." I woke up cranky, wondering, *What the heck am I doing here with **these** people?* I still didn't see myself as one of them—these Jesus freaks.

I went through the first two days in a haze, and all I wanted to do was sleep. On day three, there was a session on life purpose taught by Dr. John Stanko. That session was amazing. Dr. Stanko did a **DISC** profile for me, which assesses four behaviours, i.e. dominance, influence, steadiness and conscientiousness. It revealed that my two strongest behaviours were a High **D** and a High **I** (D relates to the dominant type; the strengths of a **D** are administration, leadership, and determination). I learned the challenges for a **D** (or what I call over-played strengths) are typically being impatient, insensitive, and a poor listener.[2]

Thankfully, those behaviours are to some extent counter-balanced by my high I, which represents more of an influencer personality. Those strengths include persuading, enthusiasm, and entertaining. The challenges or overplayed strengths are inattention to detail, a short attention span, and poor follow-through. It was like a lightbulb had gone off, and

---

[2] DISC is a behavioural assessment developed in 1926 and used the world over.

it suddenly made sense as why a law career was not for me.

The characteristics that lend themselves well to law are steadiness and compliant behaviours, both of which were my lesser strengths. What really blew me away was that the dominant type had value. For many years I had tried to mute my D behaviours since my tendency to organise was labelled as being bossy, my determination as intense (a polite way of saying I bullied people into doing things), and my leadership ability was seen as arrogance or wanting the limelight. This profile's insight gave me a new window with which to view who I was. I did not have to hide who I was, thus being invisible or at least disguised as to my true personality. I could be visible and step up and out to be who I truly was (and am).

As I went back to my room for some rest before the evening sessions, I was on fire. I felt energised and the haze of the previous few days was gone. My roommates, two lovely older ladies, were there and we sat on our beds chatting. That afternoon those women poured into me. I had not known them before turning up and being assigned a room (I didn't get to choose because I booked late), but they seemed to know me as if Jesus was speaking to me through them. That afternoon, I had an encounter with the Spirit of Jesus and He became very, very real. In a sense, I stopped being invisible to God as well, and approached Him not as I thought I was supposed to be, but as who I was.

In that one encounter, I knew my life had changed. It was as if He was promising the more I got to know Him, the more He would reveal to me who I am along with who He is. I was beginning to find myself in Him as I came to the realisation that God created and accepts me exactly as who I am with my passions, personality, and purpose.

DISCOVERING THE REAL ME—BEING VISIBLE

I remember starting the MBA and thinking that I was going to enter the corporate world and become an executive. First, I had to master some things, since I needed a different skill set if I was going to be a leader. I was correct, but not in the way I thought.

The MBA was challenging for me in many ways. I had to confront subjects that frankly, after secondary school (high school), I had hoped I would never revisit, which included math. I would also have to study statistics and finance. Not only did I believe I was inept at these subjects, I also feared them. Let me explain how real my fear was. I recall attending a senior lawyers meeting while with my firm in Camden. We were reviewing the financial statements and I couldn't make head nor tail of them. I was so afraid that I felt like my heart was coming out of my chest. I tried hard to focus, and it was then that I realised I had the profit-and-loss sheet upside down.

It struck me that if I was going to be a leader, I had to master various things that were foreign to me, and finance was one of them. Not only did I have to read financial statements in my MBA program, but I also had to learn about return on Investment, arbitrage, and all sorts of other financial theories and analysis. If I didn't do that, I would become invisible because my co-workers would not take me seriously and would look past me as a colleague and professional.

I started spending extra time on finance and statistics, but they weren't getting any easier. One day, I was at a cocktail function and my finance tutor was there. He asked if I had collected my latest results and I said I had, while hanging my head because they were not great. He said, "You know you can do this. I can see you love to analyse and that's all we're asking." He continued, "Think of the financial statement as a picture. Treat the numbers like clues. You're trying to understand the story behind the numbers."

That revolutionised my thinking and on my next assignment, I was among the top three students, along with the accountants in the group. I couldn't believe it. Having the right perspective is everything. I went from believing, "I'm just not a numbers person" to realising I had placed limitations on myself due to fear. I stepped up and out where finance and statistics were concerned. Not only did my confidence with numbers grow, but later in my career I taught a statistics class and designed and taught a programme "Finance for Non-Financial Managers." Now that is truly becoming visible having been the opposite for so long.

My MBA was a journey in personal discovery and development. In fact, part of the programme was designed to be just that because we had to take a weekly personal development class. Most students, especially the corporate types, thought this class was a waste of time. I could understand why they felt like that because they were mainly in the distance learning programme and were working and studying. For me, however, those classes were a lifeline. They challenged my thinking, not just about how my values aligned or misaligned with the corporate way of doing things and with the leadership paradigm I was seeing, but the classes also caused me to reflect on how I saw myself and other people.

In one of the classes, we each took the Myers Briggs Type Assessment.[3] I was excited to see what it would reveal having recently completed my **DISC** assessment. I found out that I exhibit the **ENFJ** personality traits Extroversion (**E**), Intuition (**N**), Feeling (**F**) and Judging (**J**). We were all given our individual results with no description or idea as to what the letters meant. Then the trainer split the room into eight sections, each representing an MBTI type indicator, with extroversion and introversion being in opposite corners of the room.

---

[3] The Myers-Briggs Type Indicator® (MBTI®) is a personality inventory that is based on the psychological types described by C. G. Jung. The essence of the theory is that much seemingly random variation in the behavior is actually quite orderly and consistent, being due to basic differences in the way individuals prefer to use their perception and judgment. MBTI is not considered a robust instrument concerning personality type – psychologists use the "Big 5" as the standard for personality assessment. See,' John, O. P., & Srivastava, S. (1999). *The Big-Five trait taxonomy: History, measurement, and theoretical perspectives.* In L. A. Pervin & O. P. John (Eds.), Handbook of personality: Theory and research (Vol. 2, pp. 102–138). New York: Guilford Press.

We were asked to note the first type in our overall profile and head to that corner of the room. I was not particularly surprised to learn the behaviours of an extrovert since it correlates to the High **I** on the **DISC**. Nor was I surprised by the people who stood with me in the group of extroverts, or seeing who was standing in the introverted quadrant. Things got a little more surprising, however, as we went through the second, third, and fourth type Indicators in our profiles.

I remember distinctly hearing people in the room gasp when I headed to the feeling section. It was more astonishing to see the people with whom I was standing. These were the people everyone perceived as gentle, caring, and relational, something I was not perceived to be; Given the challenges I mentioned earlier that high **D**s are considered to be insensitive, impatient, and poor listeners. Whilst even then I would not have described myself as a poor listener, I was definitely labelled by others as insensitive and impatient.

The feeling type indicator, by the way, is the opposite to the thinking type indicator. A characteristic of the thinking type is when making decisions to prefer to look first at logic and consistency as opposed to the feeling type that tends to look first at the people and special circumstances. The thinking characteristics lend themselves well to being a lawyer. I couldn't believe I was an **F** type and not a **T** type. After all, I was a lawyer and it was second nature for me to use logic and analyse—or so I thought.

After the class, we had a one-on-one coaching session. I asked my coach how did I get an "F" since I had always been perceived as "hard." I even shared with her my DISC profile and the fact that I am a high **D** and high **I**, and the **D** behaviour is not known for being empathetic or caring. My coach noted that my I score on the DISC profile was higher than my **D** score. She also reminded me that it's about the *way* I make decisions, not the *outcome* of those decisions. I didn't quite understand this until later, but that day I was relieved. I felt like she was saying "I see you." I wasn't invisible to her, even though I was still learning to see myself. Just like the scene in the *Avatar* movie (if you've seen it) where Neytiri sees human Jake for the first time and says "I see you."

A key takeaway for me was learning to live into who I was created to be. Irrespective of whether you have a faith, do you feel you are not here by accident—that there is a bigger purpose for you than eating, sleeping, working, and having fun?

CONNECTION REQUIRES AUTHENTICITY

This chapter described self-awareness, which is getting to know ourselves, and, how our unique characteristics impact others. As leaders we must know who we really are, and that includes our passions, personality, purpose, and principles (governing values). This not only keeps us anchored when tough decisions or conflicts arise, but it's essential for building relationships of trust, which lead to connection with other people.

Think of it this way: Could you have a relationship with a person who is invisible? Of course not! Yet, that is what we try to do when we act like someone we are not, and then ask people to get to know us. It's impossible, until we stop being invisible and step up to the truth of who we are, and step out to relate to others and our work in that reality.

CHAPTER 4
LEADERSHIP: WHAT DOES IT TAKE?

"Ability is what you're capable of. Motivation determines what you do. Attitude determines how well you do it."
- Lou Holtz, former American football player, coach, and television analyst.

After I finished my MBA, I went to work full-time at my job as a practice manager. It was at a small firm and I was being given more and more responsibility in terms of running the practice and having input into decisions at the partner level. I loved the job and my validation came when I was offered partnership. I was the only non-practicing partner, which was unusual, and this boosted my confidence significantly. This was not because of the title but because I was recognised for doing a good job as a manager rather than a practising lawyer. At the time, it was also recognition that I was a leader, even though I didn't see myself as a leader then. I was purposed for leadership, but I was invisible—to myself and others. I learnt much about leadership in that role.

You may be like I was, unsure if you are a leader or not. You may be asking yourself questions like, "What does it take to be a leader?" or "How will I know I'm a leader?" I became fascinated with leadership, and began looking into the competencies leaders needed. As a practice manager, I was not only seeing in other leaders the things I was reading, but began to apply them myself, sometimes successfully but oftentimes not.

For example, a key competency for a leader is *managing change*. I knew little about managing change beyond the theories I had read. The firm was changing rapidly. We had a big vision to grow and to do so, we had to do things differently. Lawyers by nature are somewhat risk-averse and prefer steadiness over change—then again, so do most people. As we started to make the changes, we engaged the whole firm. No one was left out, no matter at what level they worked.

I conducted workshops and seminars, and even partnered with a new firm that had designed a game to help teach lawyers about the business of running a law firm. That was a fun day as we saw teams competing to win by using innovative strategies to grow their fictitious firm. Not only did people's awareness increase that it was not enough just to be good lawyers, their sense of collaboration and the feeling of being in it together, not just as a team but a family, also increased. The latter characteristic, however, had its challenges.

Several people were struggling with the changes. The changes required the lawyers to be more administrative because the firm did government legal aid cases and the government was seeking greater accountability and transparency concerning how funds were being spent. One senior lawyer in particular refused to even try different things, let alone comply with the new procedures. This lawyer was liked by clients but was not delivering the way she needed to, or at the level she was capable of. Her supervising lawyer had tried all kinds of performance techniques to help her improve, but this was really a case of "won't do," not "can't do." Finally, it was suggested I try since I have a more direct approach.

I organised a formal meeting with the lawyer and I explained why we were meeting straight off the bat and went through her recent performance information. I asked her what she thought was the problem. She began a tirade of being unable to work in the environment because the changes did not represent the values she thought the firm had originally, and she went on and on. I asked her if she was unhappy working in the firm and she said yes, to which I said, "Well, things are changing. You have a choice to adapt and change as we are all having to or go somewhere that better aligns with what you want and will make you happy. It's your choice."

If I had stopped there, it would have been a productive session. Instead, I continued to speak about her need to take responsibility for her life and stop blaming others. We had been close at one time and I used examples of things in the lawyer's private life, not just work. What I said was true, but that wasn't the point. It was too much, too soon, and in the wrong setting. I had violated her trust as a friend and had no authority (permission) to be telling her what her problem was.

When we tell someone about their behaviour, they may not be ready to hear it—so we better make sure we have authority (permission) to call them out on it. That comes from a relationship of trust and I had just broken that so there was no way it was going to be well received. Moreover, what's the point of simply telling someone about their behaviour if we don't take time to help them process that information and come to a solution? I had neither suggested a process nor did I provide any solution.

The lawyer wrote a letter of complaint and sought to imply constructive dismissal, but there were no grounds. Nonetheless, it got ugly and was tough for all in the firm. Up until the time the lawyer left, not only did her performance drop even more significantly, but she was hostile to all the partners. She played the victim so colleagues took the view that she had been badly treated. It was a hard lesson for me to learn, which was: *It's not enough to get the job done; how we get the job done matters too.* I have to confess, I didn't understand the full extent of the lesson until much later in my career.

This story not only demonstrates that leaders don't always get it right, but more importantly for me, it caused me to ask myself some searching questions. It is this ability to reflect on our own behaviour and make decisions to change, grow, and improve that are the starting points for leadership. It is self-leadership, for you cannot lead others if you have not mastered leadership of self.[4]

Self-leadership requires us to deliberately grow as individuals, which is a phrase that defines personal development. It's not just about changing your behaviours, but also changing your inner life (attitudes and beliefs) so you can be more effective. The truth is, leadership *is* about transformation—first personally and then influencing transformation in others. This is frightening but exciting at the same time. Keep in mind that transformation is not the same as change.

For example, you get a promotion to manager and instantly you are no longer one of the guys or girls, and that represents a change. On the other hand, the process of learning to lead your friends and peers requires a radical alteration of your mindset as well as behaviours. That transition process leads to transformation. That is the reason leadership is a

---

[4] A great book on self-leadership is Bryant, A. and Kazan, A.L., (2012), *Self-Leadership: How to Become a more Successful, Efficient and Effective Leader from the Inside Out*. The authors define self-leadership as "the practice of intentionally influencing our thinking, feeling and behaviours to achieve our objectives."

journey not a destination. It's also the reason why experience counts since you learn through experience. I started my leadership journey during my MBA, but little did I know there was much more to come.

LEADERSHIP COMPETENCIES

The quote by Holtz at the start of this chapter is the best description of what leaders, and for that matter any employee, needs. He defined ability as what you are capable of doing. Most organisations determine what you are capable of by assessing a new hire or employee against a set of competencies, a cumulative term for knowledge, skills, and behaviours required to perform in a job. When I started out as a leader, there was much emphasis on competencies like:

- strategy/strategic planning;
- finance;
- people management, especially performance management.

Later on, the focus seemed to shift to what was typically known as the "softer skills" like

- change management & culture;
- communication;
- coaching and mentoring.

Holtz was right in that no matter what competencies you possess, your motivation determines what you actually do—and I would add how you do it. Your attitude then determines how well you do it. In my experience, factors like motivation and attitude are just as important as the ability competencies, especially attitude, since this is considered by some to be a critical component of character.

Dr. Ron Jenson, in his book *Achieving Authentic Success,* developed ten principles to build character that are split into three categories: attitude, beliefs, and commitments. Character emanates from a leader's values and principles, but starts with having the proper mental state (attitudes).

Principles provide universal moral truths and these provide a strong basis for developing one's character. This is important because people follow leaders they trust and who exhibit a strong moral imperative. The good news is character can be developed.

Unlike knowledge and skills, which are relatively easy to obtain from programmes like the MBA, character is much more difficult to develop, but well worth the effort. During my leadership journey, I have had to question if I am of good character. I thought I was, but I found the values I thought I had did not always show up in my leadership or at other times in my life.

For example, I have always sought to put people first, which is consistent with my primary behaviour trait as a high **I** personality. My secondary trait is a high **D**, however, and I like to drive projects and see results. It is easy to put people first when they are being cooperative, but when they become a stumbling block to achieving results, my approach was, *if you can't change the people, then change the people.* Let me explain further with another of my life stories.

I was once leading a large-scale transformation programme in the public sector. We were not achieving the results as planned and a major reason was one department, instrumental to the transformation agenda, seemed unable to implement key projects. I was assigned the role of troubleshooter to work with the department and get the projects back on track. The director, whilst in the post a while, was not strong in the relevant technical area and had little experience. Part of the reason I was assigned to monitor the department was because it was an area of strength for me and I had significant experience.

Typical of my high I style, I tried to make things happen by inspiring the people, using the vision for transformation and pointing out the importance of their contribution. Whilst that worked to some degree, there was a need for more and faster action. I spoke to the director about alternative strategies, but these were not well received. Despite the old adage of "doing the same things and expecting different results is madness," the director persisted in pursuing the old ways. Pressure was on me to deliver and my secondary behaviour trait, the high **D**, kicked in. I became more directive since I owned the transformation agenda as a whole.

I therefore made recommendations to the oversight committee and persuaded them to take a different course of action. The challenge was the director, who had not bought into the recommendations, was ordered to implement them and that person had neither the technical skill nor motivation to do so. After a few weeks, things were at a stalemate because the director refused to communicate with me. The oversight committee asked me, "Would things move more quickly if we changed the director?" The simple answer was yes.

We then had a meeting with the director about the change, but it was not well received. My focus was on getting the results, so we pressed forward with the transition, handling it my way. Changing the director turned out to be a disaster because despite my best advice, the candidate who transferred in was even weaker than the previous director. In the end, I was given the project to manage directly with a small team. We achieved the results, but I felt a deep sense of remorse when it was over.

I realised that I had not put people first which is an issue of character, and does not align with my personal values of collaboration (which includes support, encouragement, and accountability). I did not focus on the director's needs and how I could serve her. I could have had a coaching conversation with her and been honest about the challenges I had observed and offered to help her overcome them. I also could have taken more time to help the director understand why the strategies they were trying were not optimal and why the new ones were preferable.

The director came from an IT background and had a

high need for structure, and I could have sought to provide that. I did none of these things because my focus was on results as opposed to developing people. Of course, I may have done all that and the director could still have dug her heels in and refused to cooperate or implement the new strategies. In fact, I suspect that is what would have happened, but it is irrelevant because I did not even try. As I stated before, it is not just about getting the job done; it is about *how* we get the job done.

This was a painful lesson for me and something I deeply regret to this day. I reflected on how my values had not aligned with my actions and I asked myself what I was going to do about it. I spent time reclarifying and describing my personal-values framework and set about reviewing my decisions and actions against them on a weekly basis. I still use the same tag line, *if you can't change the people, then change the people,* but my approach has changed. I spend much more time working to change limiting mindsets while helping people change their attitudes and beliefs so they can be more productive. I resist my first reaction to consider them a stumbling block that needs to go. I can't say I'm fully there yet, but my character and wisdom are developing.

MOVING FROM FEAR TO BELIEF

No one is ever ready to lead. Even if you are purposed for leadership, the reality is always different than what you expect. I have worked with and spoken to many leaders and our most common fears are criticism, failure, and assuming responsibility.

My earlier experiences with my bar finals cured me of my fear of failure. As for assuming responsibility, I took on much responsibility early in life after my parents divorced when I was six years old. The one fear I did not overcome until much later, however, was fear of criticism, which I saw as rejection. That led to me to play it safe at times, only to become frustrated. Then I took bigger risks than I might otherwise have done had I operated from a place of authenticity in the first place, since innovative thinking and new approaches are normal characteristics of my work. I learnt the only way to overcome my fears was when the pain of not overcoming became greater than the fear itself. For me, living like an invisible woman by playing it safe was no longer an option.

Completing the DISC and MBTI were transformative for me. They helped me to better understand my personality including my strengths and over-played strengths, which is when a strength taken to the extreme actually becomes a weakness. For example, my fear of rejection was rooted in my people-centred strength as a high I. When this strength is overplayed, however, it can become manipulation of others. I learned that, although it is difficult for us to change our natural behaviours, we can learn to moderate and adapt them and thus use another behaviour that may be more appropriate to a situation. To do this, I had to have sufficient self-awareness. Self-awareness includes what we know about ourselves—the parts we see, the parts we hide, and the parts we cannot see.[5]

The JoHari window is a great tool for creating self-awareness from feedback. It has four quadrants, two of which are about self (things you know about yourself and what others know about you) and two that are unknown to you (but others may know them). With this tool and the help of friends and colleagues, I became much more self-aware, especially concerning my blind spots. For example, one of my blind spots was the fact that I thought I was always highly organised. As my business grew and I had to balance leading multiple projects at the same time, however, I struggled. I knew I was struggling but the reason was not clear. My little sister, Chinwe, the fourth Musketeer, came to intern with me one summer and after a

---

[5] "Personality refers to individual differences in characteristic patterns of thinking, feeling and behaving. The study of personality focuses on two broad areas: One is understanding individual differences in particular personality characteristics, such as sociability or irritability. The other is understanding how the various parts of a person come together as a whole." Adapted from the Encyclopedia of Psychology http://www.apa.org/topics/personality/ [accessed 12/09/2017]

week said, "You are great at what you do, but horrible at time management." She showed me how I repeatedly made appointments without checking my diary and how I always underestimated my workload.

She decided she was going to take over managing my diary and, during meetings, she would prompt me not to answer immediately if asked when I could deliver on a client requirement. She had me say I would get back to them by the close of the day with a schedule of deliverables. From that point on, I decided to stop overseeing the project management on my consulting assignments. I now include in all my assignments the role of project manager who happens to be a close friend and colleague, and she manages the projects for me. She is integral to my success—and my sanity.

We all need to be and feel validated for who we really are or for what some call our authentic selves. It's so important to have "good people" as we say in the Caribbean; people like my sister, who will tell the truth in love, along with what we do well and what we don't do well. They come alongside to help us get better. We all need others who will support, encourage, and hold us accountable. I have made it a priority to have such people in my life, both professionally and personally.

I've learned that it doesn't matter if others validate me unless I first accept myself, both the good and the bad. How did I do that? By coming to realise that God loves and accepts me, and gave me my personality and purpose to use. Then I started to believe I could be a leader, since I could see and admit what I was good at. I could see my potential and how it could grow, as long as I was willing to learn and be teachable. You guessed it: I had to be visible and then step up and step out. It is simple to say and write, but not simple to do.

I'll end with this humorous story about blind spots. I grew up in Manchester, a city in northern England. I went to a small, close-knit Catholic primary school, which for those not familiar with the English school system, runs from age five through eleven. I loved school and learning, and was always asking questions and then more questions. As is typical in the U.K., at the end of the school term, we had school photos taken. I sat proudly with my classmates in a pretty dress and had my picture taken—a picture I cherished.

During primary school years, my parents separated and we moved from Manchester to London with my dad. It was a tough time but I made friends easily and continued to enjoy school. By the time I was eleven, I had some good friends. One of them, Debbie, had come to my house for dinner. This was typical, for our house was a revolving door for friends, family, and children of different cultures and colours. I wanted Debbie to see how much I'd changed since leaving primary school. We flipped through old family photos and there was the picture from my Catholic primary school. I excitedly asked, "Guess which child is me? Bet you can't guess."

My friend stared at me as if I had lost my mind. "Really, what do you mean 'guess'?"

I said, "I don't think you'll be able to spot me because I've changed so much."

Debbie responded, "Seriously, you're the only black child in the photo."

I was stunned because all those years I had never noticed I *was* the only black child in my school photo or in my class. I had not known what it was to feel different because of my colour. For me, I was like everyone else, and clearly blind to the obvious.

The point is that when we lead from our authentic self, we stop being invisible—to ourselves and to others.

- What are your values? Can you articulate them? Do you apply them in your daily life?
- In what ways have you made yourself invisible by leaning into other's expectations or perceptions of you that may not necessarily be true? Why not try a personality tool like MBTI or

DISC to reflect on whether your natural tendencies align with what you think or if they have been skewed or impacted by what others think?

> **MORAL CHARACTER BUILDS TRUST THAT LEADS TO CONNECTION**
>
> This chapter describes the competencies that relate to moral character, which are more important than the technical skills. People may not appreciate our leadership style or agree with our way of doing things, but if we demonstrate strong moral character, they will trust and follow us. This is likeability, not charisma, and it leads to connection.

CHAPTER 5
LABELS: IT'S ALL ABOUT IDENTITY

*"Your identity is your
most valuable possession – protect it."*
– Elastagirl, *The Incredibles*

One of the earliest labels we all have is our name. When I was five years old and about to start big school, I was quite excited. My dad asked me under what name I wanted to be registered. I said of course my Nigerian name of NKECHI. My dad tried to tell me that might not be so easy, but nonetheless if that's what I wanted, he would proceed. I said it was, having no clue what he was talking about.

My first day of school came and as they read the children's names out, I was eagerly expecting mine: Nkechi Okosi.

I heard a stutter then a half attempt at "Nuh Ketchi" and I shouted, "Me! It's Nkechi." Then I became angry as the teacher tried to pronounce Okosi and the class laughed. I asked her to stop and pronounced my surname for all to hear. Then I said, "You can call me Felicia." That incident is burned in my memory for life. It was the start of me being invisible, since up to that point, I had never used the name Felicia and barely knew how to spell it.

Names are important because they give us identity. I love that the meaning of my name Felicia reflects my personality: happy, joyful, and optimistic. I am also proud of my Nigerian name for it speaks to my heritage and reminds me that I am a gift from God, especially on those days when I struggled to know and then believe in who I am. My birth was not an accident, nor was anyone else's.

Because of my personality, I was given many labels: Rebel, Risk-Taker, Independent, Oreo, Chatterbox, Harsh, and others. I'm sure you have your own set of labels too. The old child's rhyme "sticks and stones may break my bones, but names will never hurt me" is such rubbish. There is nothing more painful than being called names that label, especially by people you trust and whose opinion you value. Often the labels we give ourselves are much worse than the labels others give us.

I remember being at university and struggling to fit in. As I wrote before, I wasn't like most of the other girls who were demure or some version of it. I had a passion for learning, but often felt I didn't understand. When I was a child, I was labelled a chatterbox or told to stop showing off because I asked and answered lots of questions in school. I was at the place where it was all about learning and I needed to know, so during every lesson I was the one asking questions, especially in my legal trusts class.

The other students groaned, for every question I asked generated more questions since the lecturer's answers never really helped further my understanding. Therefore, no class session ever finished on time. Every week, I dreaded the class because I felt I was dumb. It seemed like everyone else clearly understood since they weren't asking questions. Then one day, after a rather intense round of asking and answering questions where it was clear even the lecturer was fed up with me, we all left the class, late as usual. Simon, a student everyone considered to be the top student, said to me rolling his eyes, "Felicia, stop asking F****** questions. No one understands his class; he's a bad teacher. We'll just have to read up on it ourselves." That incident was a godsend, for right then and there, he debunked the label that I had started to form about myself: I was not that bright, and maybe even dumb.

BEING MISUNDERSTOOD

Waldo Emerson said, "to be great is to be misunderstood." I hesitate sharing this quote since I still hear the tapes from my past ringing in my ears with the words, "she's arrogant" or "she thinks she's better than the rest of us," but I've come to understand how true Emerson's statement is.

One of my favourite places is Disney's The Magic Kingdom, not so much because I love rides (which I do), but because I love the stories about Walt Disney. I even went on the Disney Business Tour—a must in my mind. Walt Disney was an animator, producer, and innovator. In 1937, Walt Disney was determined to create the first-ever, feature-length animated film, *Snow White*. There were so many doubters and critics that the project was known in Hollywood as "Disney's folly." He was often misunderstood and this was one of those times; people often can't see where leaders are going. Anyway, *Snow White* was made and the rest is history. It earned more than $8 million in revenue during its original release. That reinforced the truth that if we don't want to be average leaders but great leaders, we will be misunderstood. It's not a case of we might, we *will*.

Whilst I was doing my MBA, it became clear that unless I wanted to re-mortgage my flat again, which I didn't, I needed to get a job. Aside from needing some income, I also wanted to try out my new-found skills. As I mentioned earlier, I took up a position as a practice manager of a law firm. In essence, I would be managing the practice with the partners. I was so excited when I heard my application was successful, especially since I had made it clear I could not work full-time due to my MBA studies.

I immediately set about using my new skills by tackling a strategic assessment, doing visioning sessions, and other such activities. I quickly came to realise that the firm would not be able to grow unless it made some tough decisions, namely closing down its immigration department. I tentatively mentioned this at a partners' meeting to test the waters. The reaction was as I imagined. It was non-negotiable and I was told I didn't understand the culture of the firm if I thought that was an option. I felt like the big, bad stepmum.

A year later when the firm was struggling financially, however, I gently nudged the partners to revisit the issue again. We did and this time I actually presented a business case and the decision was made to shut down the department. I was talking to my mum about work and this particular decision when she asked. "How could you do that when lots of people will lose their jobs, some who are even friends of yours?" I responded that it was the right thing to do because if we didn't, even more people would lose their jobs. She thought, as many others have assumed, that I was being harsh.

At that moment, I remembered what my MBA coach had said about how F types make decisions based on feelings, rather than logic. In my instance, this translated to putting people first. I had recommended closing the department, and it was a tough decision. Some great people would lose their jobs, but ultimately it was so more jobs would be preserved, which was the greater good. As part of the business case, I had included steps to ensure every member of the department would receive help in finding a new job.

We tapped our networks, I helped prepare CVs and trained for interview preparation, and everyone who wanted a new job in the same field was able to secure one. I realised I had been logical in my approach, but my decision was first and foremost based on trying to save as many jobs as possible. The outcome led to people misunderstanding me, thinking I was uncaring, but in the long run, it saved the firm and many more jobs.

What I learned from that is I had to understand who I was before I could challenge the labels others sought to place on me. I had to step up to the truth and step out in the confidence of who I was, not who others thought or were saying I was. During my MBA and while becoming a practice manager, I reassessed who I thought I was. I came to the conclusion that the happy, caring person who had been struggling to get out since I was a child, was *still* struggling to get out. I had allowed others' perceptions and expectations to shape me and in doing so made myself invisible, so much so that I didn't even see me. I was afraid if I wasn't the person people expected me to be, I would be rejected, which is the basic fear of the High I style.

I graduated with my MBA and, unbeknownst to me, I was nominated for and awarded the Chartered Institute of Management's Award for *best overall contribution to the MBA programme in a supportive and constructive manner*. Not only was I discovering the real me, but others had begun to see it too. The real me was emerging.

REDEFINING ME

Even when we step into our authentic selves, it can be a daily struggle not to accept the labels or names other people place on us. Sometimes we even willingly accept labels because they seem good. As I mentioned earlier, my relationship with my dad was rocky during my time at bar school. I felt like I had not lived up to my role as the eldest daughter, and I was always particularly sensitive to that expectation. Because I am a leader, I always solved problems. I was seen as the fixer to my family and friends. I would rush to their aid, no matter what time of day.

By the time I hit my forties, this had characterised me for so long that I didn't realise I was often getting burnt out trying to live up to that label. My dad took title in Nigeria, which means a man is formally recognised as an elder and takes on the responsibilities of guiding the community—similar to an elder appointed by Moses at the recommendation of Jethro his father-in-law as described in Exodus 18.

The title-taking ceremony lasted for two weeks. During that time, the title holder selects title names of honour and affection for each of their children. My dad selected the name "Azum Dialo" for me, which when translated means "bearer of burdens." In fact, when my dad was considering this name, he consulted my stepmum to see what name she thought would be a good fit for me, and she came up with the exact same name: Azum Dialo. I was so proud of this name because it accurately characterised me—but that was part of the problem.

In 2014, a friend sent me a motivational clip to watch titled "A Time of Re-Definement." I had trouble opening the file and thought nothing more of it. Then one of my stepsisters (my sister Chinwe has sisters on her mum's side and we see each other as sisters too) sent me the same one. Once again, I couldn't open it. I'm not superstitious, but I felt it was more than a coincidence so I contacted the organisation that put it out and managed to get a link that worked. The clip spoke about "some of us needing to undergo a name change" to be re-defined. I came to realise how labels and names truly had power.

I realised I had proudly accepted my title name as my identity. I felt it was my responsibility to bear everyone's burdens. This may come across as caring and the Christian thing to do, but it is not. As a leader, one of our important responsibilities is to draw out the greatness in others. Greatness doesn't come with ease, but is developed through difficult circumstances when you must make decisions for yourself, say what you want, and in doing so, grow. I've had many of those types of circumstances in my life, and it is in those painful times that I have grown the most and found out who I truly am.

My taking responsibility for others and not allowing them to address their own challenges whilst I stood on the side lines as a cheerleader meant I was depriving them of the opportunity to grow and become great. It was such an epiphany for me. I began to deliberately choose not to 'step up to the plate', and in some circumstances I faced more misunderstanding. Many thought I had become selfish.

There were times during this part of my leadership journey when it was easier to revert to self-sufficiency rather than delegate, especially since the buck stopped with me as a leader. How many times have you "just done it yourself" because you didn't have confidence it would be done properly, if at all? (And sometimes, it's not done right *or* at all.) For those I had the privilege to lead, I gave them space to try, fail, and then push through as they met their challenges head on.

It was at this point that I realised the best thing I could learn to do was to become a coach, being someone who helped others find their own solutions whilst they took responsibility for their personal learning and growth—and that's what I did. I became a certified coach and it is one of the single biggest returns on investment I have ever experienced, both in my personal and professional life. It was not easy, however. No one likes to see people struggle, especially friends and family, but I had to learn there is only one burden bearer: our Creator.

It's time to unleash your true identity—we are never successful living as someone else.

- What labels are you allowing to shape your identity?
- As a leader, are you allowing those you lead to grow by delegating, even if it is much easier and more efficient to do it yourself?

ACCEPTING OURSELVES ENABLES US TO ACCEPT OTHERS AND IS A KEY TO CONNECTION

This chapter spoke about identity. Finding our identity starts with knowing who we really are. This can be difficult if we don't feel accepted, loved, or adequate. For me, finding out that God loved and accepted me has shaped my acceptance of myself and my understanding of who I am created to be. Acceptance is the place where our confidence comes from. When we are genuinely confident, rather than simply faking it (bravado), we can appreciate and champion others without feeling threatened or weak. That is why the strategy defined as 'fake it until us make it' will only get us so far.

CHAPTER 6
DO I REALLY HAVE TO SERVE?

"To whom much is given, much will be required"
(Luke 12:48).

I started this book by saying that leadership involves inspiring, serving, and connecting. My hope is that the stories of my journey, good and bad, have inspired you. I am not exceptional, though I am unique, and so are you. We are all one of a kind and can all fulfil our purpose if we find it, believe we can, and take action.

We all want to be an inspiration and live a life of significance. We may call it something different, like wanting to be good at something or wanting to feel validated, but they all stem from the same desire to be significant. That's why celebrity TV has become so powerful. While seeking significance is almost universal these days, wanting to serve others is a little different. Servant leadership is a much-talked-about concept, but for the most part, it is not adopted or applied in the majority of workplaces.

Let's be honest. The thought of serving others can make us recoil because we don't want to be used. Moreover, our need to be significant can compete with wanting to serve. We see service as something lowly and if we serve others, then in some way that lessens us. That's the message we see played out in the lives of many leaders today. Their thinking is, "I'm the top dog and to be successful, I must focus on me, not others," or "it's a dog-eat-dog world out there." It sounds horrible, but we've seen too many company cultures that reflect those attitudes, and there are few leaders willing to challenge or change the prevailing thinking.

GROWING GREATNESS IN OTHERS THROUGH SERVICE

I mentioned there was a time when I put results before people and would not delegate to team members, especially if I was up against a tight deadline. I simply felt it was quicker and safer if I did it myself. This was often because of my own poor planning and fear.

I now see one of my primary responsibilities as a leader is to grow others and bring out their greatness. When I worked at the law firm where I was a partner, the senior secretary was seen as difficult, to the point that the firm was considering termination if things didn't improve. I saw something in this young woman, however, and much to the partners' astonishment, I identified her as my successor.

I had a frank conversation with the secretary about her negative behaviours and impact on the firm, explaining the consequences if this continued. More importantly, I told her what I could see in her and that if she was willing, I would teach her how to use her strengths more productively. The secretary did in fact succeed me when I left and no one believed the transformation would have been possible had they not experienced it.

To grow others, we cannot micro-manage; we must delegate. This approach is an unfamiliar one in many of the contexts I work in, and I have realised, in most cases, I need to be explicit in telling my team and others my approach. For example, I was once director of a transformation project and recruited a deputy. One of the reasons for her appointment was that she had strong organisational abilities that exceeded my own as well as being technically competent.

After a few months of working together, I was surprised she was not taking initiative and running with projects and activities as I thought she would. I also noticed she was frustrated. Eventually during one of our meetings, I asked about her frustration and she replied, "I thought you were more organised." I admitted I was not but recognised that she was, and explained I had been waiting for her to step up to the plate in that regard. She confessed she had seen where she could meet the needs of the team and project, but had been concerned that since I was the leader, I might not appreciate it because it may make me look bad. I explained I would more than welcome it because my philosophy is that success is a team effort. I am happy to be supported by a capable group of people, some even more capable in certain areas than I.

Delegation prevents leaders from suffering burn out, which is inevitable when they try to do it all themselves. It also provides opportunities for growth for those we have the privilege to lead, if done intentionally and supported by coaching. Not delegating is actually a worse mischief than a leader who delegates for the sole purpose of getting others to do their work for them. In the latter scenario, the employee will gain skills, but eventually will see through the leader and either confront them or get burned out and choose to leave. There is growth, though it is painful.

If leaders choose not to delegate, however, their employees may also get fed up and leave and there will have been pain but no growth. They will likely leave more insecure in their abilities, wondering if they are good enough or capable. This is far worse than the former scenario.

One of the other ways I seek to serve my clients is supporting leaders. Oftentimes, the leaders I work with do not have the luxury of anyone serving them as a sounding board because of the nature of their work, or because they fear being seen as weak. Even though my role is usually technical and my team and I must deliver on time and to budget, I always make time and space to serve these leaders well by providing a listening ear. I describe myself as a government advisor and, whilst this is typically in a technical capacity, this other part of my role is vital and will often extend beyond the life of the project and any payment.

Servant leadership also extends to the organisation. I work predominantly with governments, and government is meant to be continuous for the benefit of the citizenry. Too often governments and other organisations thrive because of the leader and then when another leader comes in, the department may find itself in a tailspin. I seek to build organisations that are stable and secure and will continue to thrive even if current leadership moves on.

In one government where I was leading the transformation, it was clear that some key positions were not filled, and the organisation had tried unsuccessfully to fill them. Despite it not being part of the scope of my work, I developed a plan for the organisation to recruit to these posts. I helped them put in place a new, more robust recruitment strategy along with policies to support it. I went on to facilitate the assessment centres to recruit five critical posts. Many of these positions were integral to continuing the transformation efforts that my team and I had initiated.

This was not part of my brief and I took a significant

amount of criticism for this action—and met with much resistance too. Many felt it took me away from the core work for which I was contracted. I had to work extra time to ensure that I delivered on the main scope of work, as well as supporting this and other additional non-contract initiatives so the organisation could thrive. I make a point from the inception of any assignment or role I take on to identify and train up my successor. Knowledge-sharing is one of my values and this is one way I live up to that. In the past 15 years, I have never left a job or long-term assignment where I have not maintained this practice.

BUILDING COMMUNITY

It is said that leadership is a team sport. A servant leader knows this and seeks to build a community of people, all of whom are pushing towards the same vision or goal. One of the most difficult parts of my job is bringing leaders with differing and sometimes competing interests together to deliver something of benefit for all. To do this, one has to check one's ego at the door. Although I am an advisor or sometimes a programme manager, I may be responsible for the programme, but I have no formal line management responsibility for the persons through whom I must implement the programme.

It requires focus on the goal, which is transforming the public service for the benefit of the citizenry, if I am to persevere in such a position because resistance is often high and buy-in from the politicians and senior public officials are often low. For example, I was advising a government that took a decision to improve governance. Governance has become quite a buzz word over the years, but rarely is tangible evidence evident, such as greater accountability, transparency, or increased citizen participation. I advised the government to implement a policy initiative to make their decision real. When I explained what this would mean, it was rejected. It took a number of months to finally persuade the politicians to support the initiative despite the many benefits.

There was quite an unhealthy culture in that government, which is something I have noted in recent years in many countries. Instead of public officials working together with politicians for the greater good of the country, they are effectively at war and even sabotaging the plans of the political executive, despite the importance in any democracy for public officials to be impartial. In this instance, I found the resistance from the politicians was nothing compared to the resistance I met from the public officials.

The initiative required a major change in government's way of operating and required cross-ministry support and participation, even though people had previously worked in silos, busy creating their own kingdoms. I met with and sought to persuade senior public officials of the need for the initiative and to develop a strategy. I persevered and was successful because I knew if leaders came together, the initiative would not only be a success and deliver greater transparency for citizens, but would be something they could own and be proud of. Eventually, through maintaining this posture of a servant leader and despite many leaders complaining about me (articulating I was a foreigner who was meddling in their affairs) and seeking to sabotage the initiative, we were able to get a cross-functional team together to deliver the initiative.

It took more than twelve months and was such a success that the government's donor partners recognised it as being a crucial turning point that could then trigger funding, thus resulting in greater transparency. It was amazing to see how these leaders finally owned the initiative; they were proud of what we had achieved. Despite the initiative being under the programme I managed, I knew it was important for those officials to be the face of it and to get the accolades.

I was elated to be part of it and I recognised that I had grown as a servant leader. I know when I was younger, being the high I that I am, I would have wanted to be seen as the leader of the initiative and to receive credit for it. During the course of this initiative, however, a clear feeling of oneness emerged. Instead of a group of stakeholders who worked in silos, there was instead a community of people all working on the same team towards the same ends—at least for that initiative.

MY WAY OR THE HIGHWAY

One of the things that characterises the leadership we see today, especially from politicians and business people, is the stereotype that the leader makes all the decisions and no one else can contribute. I have learned from working with politicians that many have this approach—and it doesn't work. A wisdom teaching made the point that "in a multitude of counsellors there is safety." My approach to leadership has always been collaborative, while remembering that the final responsibility rests with me as the leader. This approach, however, is not always valued, so it requires confidence to lead like this.

I attended a consulting conference that included a number of workshops offering continuing professional development training and credits. In one of the workshops, we undertook a leadership exercise. We were split into groups and given a puzzle to solve as a group. Each group was also to observe the other. Then we were to nominate a leader and complete the task in 20 minutes—not much time for a group of eight consultants who were leaders in their own right. I was nominated as leader.

My approach was to work with the team to ensure everyone's voice was heard, rather than being dictatorial. On several occasions, a young woman tried to advise the group of key elements she deemed were missed. The activity was a puzzle, and we had ten minutes left and one piece remaining wouldn't fit. I had numbered the puzzle pieces and also drawn a diagram of the current configuration.

After I watched her try unsuccessfully to make herself heard, I asked the group if we could try something different. I explained I had numbered the pieces and drawn a diagram so we could easily put them back in the exact same order if needs be. Since we had been struggling for ten minutes to get this last piece to fit, I suggested we try the young woman's suggestion. They agreed and I asked the young woman to make the changes she'd been trying to tell the group to consider.

Within five minutes, she made the changes and fitted the rest of the puzzle together, enabling our team to complete within the time. During the feedback from the group that observed, it was said that there was "weak leadership" in our group. The facilitator asked why it was weak, and the majority of the group said because the leader didn't direct. The facilitator then asked if they could tell who the leader was. They unanimously said Mrs. Linch. She then asked, if they could tell without being told who the leader was, how could it have been weak? She concluded by saying that what she observed was a leader who believed in her team and stepped in to support them when needed, and managed time well. That is what servant leaders do: They collaborate and draw out all voices.

IT TAKES HUMILITY

I was made a partner at the law firm where I was a practice manager, and shortly afterwards moved on to be a trainer and lecturer in human resources at one of the U.K.'s first private universities. By then, I realised a successful leader must learn how to manage people—at least that's what I thought. The real lesson I learned as a teacher was successful leaders need to learn how to serve people well.

One of the other reasons we may find it difficult to serve as leaders is because we mistakenly think humility is weakness, which is far from the truth. It takes strength to be humble, to submit your will to another, or to let someone else shine for the greater good. It was evident after my first few months of teaching that I was born to do it. I loved sharing knowledge and trying to find ways to help students get unstuck. I harkened back to my own college and university days when I struggled, and I wanted no one in my class to ever be in that position.

Whilst teaching finance and statistics, I had two students who couldn't grasp a particular concept after three hours. I asked any of the other students if they felt they could come up and explain it more effectively. I was determined we weren't going to move on until everyone got it. After all, we were in this together.

These students were all mature men and women who were managers in their own right, so why not ask them? One student stepped forward and, after giving an example, both students got it and we moved on. After class, the student who had helped out asked if I wasn't concerned about being seen to be a poor teacher or lesser than my students. I responded it hadn't even occurred to me since my goal was to make sure everyone understood and was equipped to pass. Their success was my success. Far from being a challenge to my authority, my openness increased my popularity and interest in my classes.

I have also learned that to walk in real humility means we cannot think of ourselves as above or better than someone else, but we should also own up to what we are good at. As a leader, we are often senior in terms of organisational hierarchy, but nothing indicates more clearly that someone is a servant leader than their actions towards those who rank lower than they do. For example, I was scheduled to deliver a workshop with a co-facilitator. The organisation responsible for setting up received a list of all the resources we needed and the layout of the room. As is usual for me, I arrived early and found the room had not been set up correctly, and also needed a bit of a clean.

I contacted the coordinator with whom I had been liaising. She was embarrassed and said she would send people over. It was a Saturday and the organisation's coordinator was only able to get one staff member to come; it seemed everyone else's phones were turned off. I was grateful to the staff member who arrived and I said "we'll do it together." I proceeded to sweep and together we lifted tables and moved chairs to rearrange the large room along with the breakout rooms. As we worked, I noted that my co-facilitator was just watching us. I asked, "Are you going to help?" but got the answer, "That's not my role," as she left the room. Needless to say, I did not work with her again.

MOTIVATION TO SERVE IS A HEART MATTER

Have you ever offered to do something for someone you didn't really want to do but felt obligated? Perhaps they would think less well of you if you didn't? Maybe they have unrealistic expectations of you and you simply don't know how to say no?

You may ask, "What's wrong with acting out of obligation or wanting the approval if the outcome is the same? At least we do something for good, and we serve." I have learned that if we don't serve from a place of genuine care and concern, from a heart that is freely giving and not expecting anything in return, then people can sense it. As a leader, the impact of acting without being genuine is that we lose credibility since people don't trust us. Motives matter.

When I first moved to the Caribbean, I was acutely aware that I was not accepted. Despite my mother being from the Caribbean and my holding citizenship in her country of birth, I was continually being told, "You not from about here." This kind of resistance is to be expected when working toward transformation because it involves change, but for me, this was magnified since I was seen as a Brit who people assumed thought she knew better than everyone else. Having lived and worked in the Caribbean for more than twelve years now, I understand why that perception prevailed. I have witnessed many consultants from so-called developed countries, both black and white, deliver projects in the Caribbean and speak to the local leaders they were working with as if those officials knew nothing, had nothing to offer, and had to be told how it was supposed to be done.

In order to overcome this misconception about me, I would extend myself above and beyond what was in my contract. I would often work outside the scope of my brief and for no pay. I would take phone calls from clients late at night and on weekends to show my commitment and was hesitant to criticise initiatives I knew would likely fail (and not because they were not being done the same way as in developed countries).

I recall one such phone call from a public official whilst I was on holiday, requesting help with a document he needed the first thing in the morning. I had been urging this official to work on this document for weeks and she had advised me she didn't need my help. I supported the effort by drafting the document for them at the late stage. The official presented it with no changes as his own work. I was angry and shocked. I felt used and my husband said, "People will always flog a willing donkey. Why did you do it if you didn't want to?"

My husband's question caused me to stop and reflect, and it helped me come to a place of understanding my own inadequacies. My actions had been manipulative. I didn't act from a place of service, for in reality it was trying to gain their approval. It was not done because I genuinely wanted to serve, but once I started, I had set an expectation I felt obligated to fulfil at any cost. That was a hard lesson.

Today I choose to go over and above because I want to see my clients have success and also believe that citizens deserve better government than we are seeing today in most countries. I do this now from a heart of service and not from ulterior motives or obligation.

SPEAKING TRUTH TO POWER

As leaders, we have influence. An aspect of serving others is using that influence for good and to speak up on behalf of those who might not be able to do so for themselves.

There is much personal risk in speaking truth to power. We risk losing our jobs, credibility, and even friends. I discovered how real this aspect of being a leader was early in my career but what I didn't bargain on was that the more influence I achieved, the more responsibility I would have and the stakes would be higher. Let me explain.

As I have grown as a leader, the projects I have had the privilege to work on have become more important. I advise governments in the Caribbean on public-sector transformation. The goal is to modernise the public service to make it more efficient and effective. My work often takes me to overseas territories, which are the equivalent of a U.S. unincorporated area. A smaller country, like Puerto Rico, is part of a larger parent country, like the U.S. The relationship between the larger parent-country government and the smaller country's government can be difficult, as was seen in the media concerning the U.S. government's aid response to Puerto Rico following Hurricanes Maria and Irma in 2017.

I walk a fine line of being an advisor in the main to the smaller country's government, but also the larger parent-country's government, since my advice must be within the governance frameworks established by the dominant parent country. I am also often leading a modernisation effort, in which the main team players are public officials. I am aware that those officials often feel the politicians and the public believe inefficiency in public service is their fault. It can be challenging to attempt to lead a change team where a majority of the team is hostile to the changes, and where the same team members are also aggrieved citizens of the respective country.

On many occasions, I've had to speak truth to power concerning policies of the larger parent country and the impact they had on the smaller country. I had to do the same in reverse and speak truth to power to ministers of government in the smaller countries, where many times I was told "we will send you home." On one occasion, speaking truth to power meant they did just that and it cost me my job.

If you are to be a leader who inspires, serves, and connects, you must develop the character necessary to stand and speak up for what is right. Peter Drucker, the famed management guru, once wrote, "Management is doing things right; leadership is doing right things." In other words, you can manage resources well, improve operational efficiency, reduce expenses, and perform other necessary management practices. Leaders do the right thing, however, and that is to focus on vision, strategy, good governance, and, in my opinion, people.

KNOW YOUR VALUES

Speaking truth to power requires conviction. Conviction comes from knowing your personal values along with the universal principles you hold. If you are truly living by these, they guide your actions. They will also guide how you interact with others and where you draw the line in the sand concerning right and wrong. When I was working as a lawyer and the firm did legal aid work, which is work for the vulnerable in society for which the state pays the legal fees, each month the state sent the firm monies on account based on our estimate of how many legal aid clients we would have. Each month, we had to reconcile what they sent with what we did.

During one of my monthly reconciliations, my boss noted I was returning a significant chunk of the monies-on-account. My boss told me there was no need to do that. He explained that we had just taken on a new client and they were going to be difficult, and so we would be billing more hours. We should simply keep the money I was returning in lieu of that since we knew it was going to happen.

My boss was likely right, but I did not know when I would bill more hours for that client, or if the client would stay the course when they found out what was involved in taking a matter to court, especially if they had to take the stand and testify. I could not estimate if next month I would bill for sufficient hours to cover the monies I was sending back. I tried explaining that to my boss but he persisted. Finally, I had to respectfully say, "In short, to do it your way is stealing and I can't do that. However, feel free if you want to fill out and sign the form, but I will not." That was my line in the sand. My boss backed down and we returned the unspent money.

One last thing. Leaders speak truth to power to bring change, not to prove they are right. That means we must have credibility with and the trust of those leaders above us whom we seek to influence. Trust brings connection with others, and connection grows when we *speak the truth in love,* as the Bible labels it. That means we are not pursuing our own agenda or operating from our ego. We genuinely care to point out the error for the other person's good *and* we want to put something right for the benefit of other people.

It's difficult to speak the truth in love during times of passion. Anger, indignation, and other fiery and powerful emotions are often a good indicator of what we care about, or the injustices we seek to remedy. I've learned to let the passion settle and then approach people when I've had time to process my thoughts *and* feelings.

It's not easy being a leader. Even if you are purposed for leadership, you can't lead well if you don't show up. That means coming out of the shadows, choosing not to be invisible.

- Are you confident in your identity? How does that impact your leadership?
- Do you seek to serve those you lead? If not, why not?
- Do you do things right or are you doing the right things?
- Do you feel you are purposed for leadership? If so what will you do about it?

SUPPORT STARTS WITH SERVING

Servant leadership is a difficult concept to grasp and an even more difficult concept to live. As Robert Greenleaf said, it's a conscious choice to serve and then to lead. I grew up with the prevailing leadership paradigm that real leaders stepped out in front of the crowd, made most of the decisions, and others simply followed. The leader was the star of the show. If we are the star of the show, however, then why should people follow us? It is human nature to ask, What's in it for me? If leaders seek what is in it for them, followers will check out and simply do the minimum their jobs require. If we as leaders make supporting our team and others the focus, however, serving them rather than our own ambition or agenda, this produces engagement. People will go the extra mile for a leader who has supported them. Try it and see.

CHAPTER 7
HOLDING OTHERS ACCOUNTABLE: FINDING THE BALANCE

I grew up in a culture where taking responsibility for your actions was critical. As leaders, we must own not only our successes but also our failures and mistakes. I have tried to share the good, the bad, and the ugly with you as concerns my leadership journey. I do this not only to be authentic, but also because we learn more from our failures and mistakes than the successes.

As someone who learned early in life to take responsibility, I assumed this was a value for everyone. Nothing would frustrate me more than when I would ask a team member "Did you send the report out as I asked" only to hear a barrage of excuses if they did not. Sometimes we cannot meet deadlines, since we are all human and make mistakes—or other things take precedent. What I needed to hear, however, was not a list of excuses but an acknowledgement that it was not done—taking responsibility first and then sharing the reason why could follow. More important to me was what the person was going to do to ensure it would get done along with when. This is not how most people operate, so I thought I was justified in holding others accountable, even if they supervised me.

Often the transformation programmes I work on have an internal team, which I lead, though I'm not the hiring manager, and consequently, the lines of responsibility and accountability can be blurred. On one project, I was clearly expected to performance manage the team. I had one team member who wasn't doing her job, so I sat down with her and made clear what was required—and provided support. She continued, however, with the same excuses. I had no alternative but to escalate the matter to my boss.

I was relatively new in the position and was still "working out my boss." I explained that I had tried to support and encourage the team member, and, had advised her specifically of where she was falling short on several occasions with no improvement. Worse, she blamed others for why she ws unable to deliver, including me for not "making clear what the role fully entailed," despite the job description. I thanked her for her feedback and advised that I would review it, which I did. After another month, nothing had changed, however, and she wasn't even coming to meetings any longer, and when I challenged her to tell me the reason, there was always an excuse.

I told my boss unless she saw an alternative, it was time to release the person from the project. She agreed, and yet three weeks later, the person was still on the project. I returned to my boss and advised her that this needed to be addressed. It became clear that whilst my boss agreed with my recommendation, she did not want to be the 'bad guy' and so wanted me to be the one to end the contract. I advised my boss that I had already indicated to the team member that I was recommending she not continue on the project. Since I didn't hire the person, I could not officially end her contract and I advised my boss of that. It became clear that my boss was not prepared to do anything and the contract eventually lapsed naturally as time passed.

To grow the greatness in others, a leader must provide support, encouragement, and accountability. To provide accountability, we must have relational capital, which means people must trust us and know that we are for them. Earlier in my career if I had been confronted with this scenario, I would likely have made the decision to let that team member go much earlier and would not have tried to provide support on the many occasions that I did (I am glad I documented them). I learnt that we can't really make people take responsibility. We can only ask them to account for their behaviour, but it's their choice if they will step up and govern themselves.

The team member, though clearly under-performing and seeking to shift the blame to others whenever she could, made a valuable comment about expectations in the role. I accepted that feedback and apologised. You might ask why because it was clear she was simply trying to shift blame. Perhaps, but I've also recognised that accountability is a two-way street. Leaders who want to hold their teams accountable, without themselves submitting to the same level of accountability from them, are abusing their position.

As for my boss, years ago I would have told her that I found her inaction lacking in courage. I've learned, as I shared previously, that no one appointed me God and that, whether I'm right or not, I don't always have permission to hold others accountable. Having the title, authority, or great intentions does not give me permission; having a relationship of trust I have built up earning me relational capital does and I didn't have enough of it on this occasion.

Similarly, the team must recognise that accountability requires relational capital but even with that intact, there are ways of giving feedback that help the hearer to be receptive. Many companies have implemented 360-degree feedback assessments, but they often fail because there is no relational capital between leaders and their direct reports. Instead of people using it as an opportunity to help their manager improve, it can often be used to vent anger and frustration or use the assessment as a weapon.

LEARNING TO ACT JUSTLY

Justice is a loaded term, but nonetheless it is a key component of leadership. You may think that because of the work I did in law and now do with politicians, justice may be relevant, but question what it has to do with a leader in a business.

First, let me define justice. In essence, it's about fairness. Fairness, however, is not the same as equality. It's not popular to say this, but the reality is we are not all born equal; we have unique and different personalities, skills, backgrounds, cultures, and access to resources. That's true diversity and a rich tapestry of many colours makes life and work interesting.

For me, justice is restorative. It restores our humanity and makes us the best we can be in this world as our Creator designed us to be. More specifically, I define justice as *healing not condemnation, acceptance not rejection, and forgiveness not punishment.* This concept is vital to accountability, but let me further explain.

Healing not condemnation can be applied in several ways. As mentioned, I was a practice manager in a law firm. We did state-funded work and once failed a state audit because of errors made by the head of the largest department in the firm, which was underperforming financially. We needed to remedy the situation within ten days or lose our licence to do state-funded work.

The senior partner was angry at the head and wanted

to tell him so, especially since he had not been cooperating with the new procedures we had implemented to avoid some of the very things the audit had brought to light. In short, he wanted to lambast the head and was becoming critical of him personally as the impact on the firm, and the partners personally, would be great if we did not pass the audit. I asked him to allow me to handle it. We met with the head, and I explained we had ten days to remedy the situation and asked, "What do you think we need to do?"

He was surprised since he came into the meeting in a defensive posture, expecting a grilling. He paused and said, "We could go back over the entries and fix them, ensuring all the details are there." I asked, "How long will it take?" He responded, "More than ten days but my team and I know it's important, so we'll get it done." After he left, the senior partner commented on how the head had never been that cooperative. Taking the approach to bring healing (remedy) to a situation moved us forward and focused us on restoring the firm to its correct position—of being in compliance.

Despite this commitment from the head, the senior partner said, "But we still have to tell him he jeopardised the firm and we need to do something like giving him a warning at least." I asked "Why? Is the intent to punish him or to ensure he doesn't do it again?" The partner was silent and then said, "The latter, but that's why he must be told, because his actions had and have consequences. He's been deliberately failing to comply with the new procedures and they were designed to stop this thing from happening."

I agreed but added, "Let's look at it from his perspective. He signed up to be a lawyer and thinks all this administration is a waste of his time, when he has clients who are facing difficult circumstances that require urgent attention. He thinks administration is beneath him, but we have to meet him where he's at if we want him and his team to buy in to the new procedures."

I had learned to put myself in another person's shoes and that helped me be empathetic. This was in sharp contrast to the incident in the past where I had the performance management conversation with another lawyer who was struggling with the changes and ended up leaving. In this instance involving the audit, I chose to accept the lawyer for who he was and took time to understand his viewpoint.

More importantly, I chose to focus on the situation at hand, and not on him personally as the problem. When we address the person, rather than the situation or challenge, people often feel like we are attacking them. I believe at the heart of this is fear of rejection; it's as if we are saying to people they are not good enough, or they are inadequate and therefore we are rejecting them. Rejection produces powerful negative emotions because we all have a basic human need to feel acceptance. It's what Maslow described as belonging, the second most important need in our needs' hierarchy after survival needs (food and shelter). We cannot belong unless we are accepted.

I should add that I didn't leave it there with the head. It was not the time to address the lawyer's resistance to change regarding the initiative and in any event, neither the senior partner nor I had the relational capital to do so since we did not manage the head. We met with the head again after he and his team remedied the errors. They worked long nights to get it done, and I expressed my gratitude. I also expressed my intent for the meeting: to discuss performance more directly and how we could move forward having learned from the incident, acknowledging it was a costly one.

This was a *forgiveness not punishment* approach. To my surprise, the head immediately took the lead and apologised. He said he had not recognised the importance of the procedures we had put in place and explained how he and his team would improve as we moved forward.

Forgiveness is not acceptance of wrongdoing; it's a

heart posture focused on restoration rather than punishment.

Over the years, I have learned to recognise that if we truly want to manage performance, then we need to recognise it's about helping those we have the privilege to lead to be better. In short, it's another element of service and requires relationship, not a lengthy process of checking and monitoring that in most organisations sends the message, *We don't trust you*. Leaders who are not hiding are secure in themselves and so have the courage to give and receive feedback often and in time, which means they immediately address situations as they arise, or bring correction. This is always with a view to helping the individual learn and improve.

BUILDING CULTURES OF HONOUR

Justice in leadership is about fairness, but it's also about how we treat each other, keeping in mind that we are all human with different quirks, faults, and vulnerabilities. Nevertheless, we must honour each other. Acting justly builds a culture of honour in an organisation. To honour you, I don't have to agree with your views, I just need to respectfully allow you to air them. If I honour you, I don't have to accept your behaviours, but I must respectfully communicate to you my own boundaries and values and what I am prepared to tolerate. In short, a leader honours a person by accepting them as a fellow human being and thus treating them as they would wish to be treated. That is referred to as the Golden Rule. A culture of honour is necessary if leaders are going to manage the diversity in our workplaces.

Let me give another example. Whilst at the bar, I was sent to do the first hearing of a young man accused of rape. As a woman and one who has experienced sexual abuse, I read the brief and frankly was angry even before I arrived at court. As I sat on the train heading to work, I thought about justice and what it meant to me. I thought about how I ought to treat this young man that would represent justice.

When I arrived, I greeted him without attitude and

listened to him. He wished to enter a plea of not guilty. That was the hard part, since in my book, *No always means no*. That day, however, I chose to honour this young man by entering the plea he wished to enter and treating him as I would wish to be treated. In fact, I had much compassion for him, because he was young and had his whole life ahead of him. If convicted, his life would never be the same. I thought, *He's someone's son and no matter what, this was a tragic situation, both for the victim and for him.* He was no demon.

You might ask how this differs from the case I mentioned earlier on with the man charged with grievous bodily harm (GBH) on a child. In my mind, it doesn't. Whilst I treated the man who abused the child with the same respect, I did not want to enter his plea because I felt so strongly about what he did; perhaps I judged his crime as worse than this later rape case. I have since come to realise that I was the one who copped out. My colleague was right: A fundamental tenet of justice is that *everyone* is entitled to a fair trial, no matter what.

Moreover, the cab rank rule, which states we cannot refuse a case because of the nature of it, is designed to ensure fairness. This is to guarantee that defendants have the right to enter the plea they desire and to let the justice system do what it is supposed to. Shirking my responsibility that day was not the honourable thing to do. If you were to ask me what I would do in the same situation today, as a leader with greater maturity, I would say I would not have asked to be released.

That said I would still have left the bar because no legal system is perfect and justice, as I define it, is rarely served. The good news is that in recent years, there's been a shift in some countries towards *restorative justice*. My hope is that such reform continues, and if I can contribute in my work with governments to hasten shift, that is even better.

One area that I haven't touched on is concerning "holding onto your visibility" once you step up and out. All too often when we first emerge from the shadows, we can seek to hold so tightly to our newfound sense of ourselves that we can actually become defensive, or erroneously believe that it's showing strength to be overly dominant and not allow anyone to make us feel invisible again. I learned that this approach did not serve me well, and nowhere was that clearer than in my marriage. It is here that I learned to find the balance!

I got married on the third of May 2003 to a wonderful guy, Andrew Linch. Andrew is what I would describe as a man's man. He was married previously, and he was the traditional breadwinner. I got married in my late thirties and in my experience, I had seen too many friends and family members get married and the wife seemed to lose her sense of self and purpose. This was especially the case with women of faith as a result of erroneous teaching that wives should submit to their husbands in all things. It was as if that role was somehow synonymous with a woman losing all her personality and strength, the very thing that attracted our husbands to us in the first place. A great resource concerning this topic is Kimberly Wagner's book *Fierce Woman: The Power of a Soft Warrior*.

I was determined not to become invisible ever again, so I became overly combative in the early stages of our marriage. What I had to learn was just as I try to build cultures of honour in the places I lead, and how I respect the authority of others, I needed to do so in my own home. My husband and I learned to honour one another or put another way, "Submit yourselves to one another because of your reverence for Christ" (Ephesians 5:21). We also learned, just as I advocate in a work context, that leadership is not about title or position in a marriage. It is not about having traditionally defined roles either.

For instance, my husband deliberately chose to sacrifice his career to enable me to pursue my career as a government advisor. This means we move from country to country as my work dictates and he usually has no status to work in those countries. Becoming a so-called "house husband" takes more strength than you might imagine. He routinely had to deal with unspoken and spoken jibes like, "So you're living off your wife," or "We can see who wears the pants in that relationship." Both my husband and I learned to value each other's strengths, just as we must know and value the strengths of our team, and deploy them in the best way possible to achieve the goal or purpose. My "aha moment" is described so well in Kim Wagner's book introduction:

> Kim admits her fierceness became a source of conflict in her marriage, but the relationship dynamic totally changed when she discovered her fierce strengths could be used to encourage and inspire her husband.

All of a sudden I recognised that just as I believe that a purposed leader must connect, inspire, and serve, the same was needed in my home.

ACCOUNTABILITY IS SERVICE AND REQUIRES RELATIONSHIP.

This chapter takes a different view than normally presented concerning managing performance. The goal in performance management is to help people learn and grow, not to punish them for under-performance. Accountability is simply another aspect of service. When I did my coaching program, I learned that honour in practice involves support, encouragement, and accountability. This is easy when all is going well, but difficult to do when we have under-performing or difficult employees. Therefore, it requires us as leaders to build relationships of trust and to have relational capital. Performance management then becomes an ongoing conversation in an environment of justice and fairness that builds a culture of honour.

CONCLUDING THOUGHTS

As I conclude this book, I return to what it looks like to lead as a purposed leader, that is a leader that inspires, connects, and serves. Throughout this book, I hope I have shown what this looks like in practice.

We can *inspire* others by having the courage to "go for it," risking failure and disappointment as we demonstrate that failure is neither final nor fatal, and by demonstrating courage, even if that means quitting.

We can *connect* with others when we become self-aware and courageously be who we were created to be by living authentically and accepting ourselves, thus giving others permission to do the same. Authenticity is critical because without it, we cannot build the moral character that those we lead need to see if they are to trust us.

Finally, we *serve* others by providing support, encouragement, and accountability, recognising that whatever we do is for the benefit of those we lead, not for punishment or our own agenda.

IS IT EASY TO INSPIRE, CONNECT, AND SERVE OTHERS?

I have always found *connecting* with others easy. Being a high I (influencer) and an F on the Myers-Briggs Type indicator, I love people and make decisions based on feelings. I learnt early on that if I was to steward this relational gift well as a leader, I had to become a purposed leader, one who has an innate sense of wanting to achieve a goal or purpose bigger than I was for the benefit of others, while not becoming manipulative, i.e. using people to achieve my own agenda. As the saying goes, we must "value people and use things."

I have learned to *inspire* others in the ways I have described above, but also by understanding the importance of having a vision as a leader and casting that vision so others are inspired and will join the work. For me or any leader, vision is not "*fluff.*" It's painting a picture and envisioning the possibilities, and to inspire others, we must also put "feet to vision," as my friend and coach, Jenni Catron, likes to say.

People follow leaders whom they trust. In the book by Stephen M.R. Covey, *The Speed of Trust,* I learnt that trust is made up of two component: credibility and competence. Competent leaders put feet to vision, which means they translate the vision through strategies and actionable plans. It's not enough to be great at connecting or being relational. Whilst I didn't focus much in this book on technical skills, the reality is that as purposed leaders, we must take time to learn our craft, and that includes understanding and applying strategy, planning, and finance. All of these are critical to putting feet to vision.

The last component, *serving* is the component I

struggle most with. There was a time I used supporting and serving interchangeably. I've learnt, however, they are different and distinct. I support those I lead because my heart is to help people grow, especially the next generation of leaders. I love to identify potential leaders, especially those who are making themselves invisible or being overlooked by others. I love nothing more than to pour into them and see them grow into who God created them to be. Serving, whilst it includes support (care, help, and encouragement) is much, much more. It includes accountability, forgiveness, trustworthiness, and humility.

I've found learning to serve the hardest of all. It places me as a leader in the tension of a seeming contradiction, which is comprised of being strong, being able to guide others, speaking truth to power, and developing the moral character that enables me to do the right thing and act with integrity even in the most difficult circumstances. Yet, serving also requires me to be humble—able to take a back seat while letting my team shine, doing tasks I may perceive as "beneath me," and on more occasions than I might like, demonstrating grace by not reacting even when someone is trying to belittle me!

Let me give one final story before I close on why I find it difficult to serve and walk in humility. Once I was programme manager for a large-scale government transformation. A member of my team had applied for the same role and as time progressed, it was clear he felt the tasks I was giving him were beneath him. He also felt he could do a better job than I, so much so that when I gave a direction or instructions, he would say, "Yes, noted," and then totally ignore what I said.

Worse than that, on one occasion, we had discussed how to deal with a situation on a project he had been leading. The deliverable was not up to standard despite much back and forth with the client. We were to meet the client and agree on a strategy focusing on the critical deliverable that had not been delivered to standard, rather than on one of the minor deliverables that were also completed. I sent out notice prior to the meeting that the focus would be on the critical deliverable as agreed. To my irritation, the project manager sent a further email to the client and key stakeholders contradicting me, and I was furious. I wanted to retaliate publicly and embarrass him—but I didn't.

Instead, I took time to calm down. The next day, I picked up the phone and called, explaining I was not getting into a "turf war" since I was the lead. I confirmed that we had agreed on a course of action and he said, "That's true." He proceeded to offer many excuses for why this or that happened to which I simply replied, "Be that as it may, it's your responsibility. It was our team's responsibility that the deliverable was not up to scratch and we must address this." He again agreed and I believed the matter to be settled, asking him to email the client and others to advise as to what we had yet again agreed. This did not happen and he proceeded to email everyone to the contrary to what we had agreed.

As the leader, I had two choices. I could let the meeting go ahead and embarrass him in front of key stakeholders, something I confess I have done in the past with difficult team members (which that could lead to a confrontation in front of the client.) Or let him run the meeting as he wished to do, which would impact his credibility and moreover irritate the client and waste their time. I decided neither course was acceptable, so I cancelled the meeting. I chose to be gracious by suggesting another method for how to address the matter of the deliverable, without publicly embarrassing the project manager. This option would still get the job done, while I once again addressed the issue as a matter of performance with the project manager. Only this time the consequences were more severe because he was on contract.

It took a great deal for me to take this approach. I had to decide to walk in humility, even if he didn't even realise it, rather than allowing my ego to react for openly showing

CONCLUDING THOUGHTS

disrespect for my leadership. How was I able to do that? Only one way, and that was by following the One whom I call "the lover of my soul." If you haven't guessed by now, I am a follower of Jesus, but even before coming to faith I recognised that leadership required more than great interpersonal or technical skills, but I didn't know what that added component was.

With experience, I have learnt that this something more is a spiritual component. It takes the leading of Holy Spirit to be a servant leader: to not react or be passive aggressive, or even confrontational; to see the good in others when 70 percent of the time they show you their worst side or seek to sabotage your efforts no matter how much grace you extend them.

My early leadership approach was to fight fire with fire, to always show my strength, use my power, and let people think I was a pushover, especially as in my line of work there are few female leaders, not to mention black ones. Or I would go completely to the opposite end and say nothing, not hold the person accountable, and become invisible. Neither was an effective way of leading, and neither was I serving that person. With the help of the Holy Spirit, I have learned to walk in humility and serve those, who by their actions, one could say didn't deserve to be served.

The Golden rule, "Do unto others as you would have them do unto you," doesn't operate only when people treat us the way we want to be treated. It's an absolute truth and guideline for behaviour no matter the circumstances, but it takes the work of the Spirit in our lives and hearts to apply. The only way I can do this is to allow God to transform my character—a work of the soul that shapes who I am as a leader.

Deepak Chopra described this process in his book, *The Soul of Leadership; Unlocking Your Potential for Greatness*, when he wrote:

> The world's great wisdom traditions all derive from a higher reality that is indescribable but can

be experienced. This is the greatest wonder and source of awe. As the ancient Indian sages declare, "This isn't knowledge that you learn. It's knowledge that you become."[6]

I don't always get it right. Sometimes I follow the leading of my ego rather than the Spirit. I am still learning to become a servant leader. What does that ultimately look like? It can best be articulated by this passage from Philippians 2 1-8:

> If you've gotten anything at all out of following Christ, if his love has made any difference in your life, if being in a community of the Spirit means anything to you, if you have a heart, if you care—then do me a favour: Agree with each other, love each other, be deep-spirited friends. Don't push your way to the front; don't sweet-talk your way to the top. Put yourself aside, and help others get ahead. Don't be obsessed with getting your own advantage. Forget yourselves long enough to lend a helping hand.
>
> Think of yourselves the way Christ Jesus thought of himself. He had equal status with God but didn't think so much of himself that he had to cling to the advantages of that status no matter what. Not at all. When the time came, he set aside the privileges of deity and took on the status of a slave, became human! Having become human, he stayed human. It was an incredibly humbling process. He didn't claim special privileges. Instead, he lived a selfless, obedient life and then died a selfless, obedient death—and the worst kind of death at that—a crucifixion (*The Message*).

---

[6] Deepak Chopra, *The Soul of Leadership: Unlocking Your Potential for Greatness* (Harmony Publishers, 2010), page 68.

FELICIA LINCH, MBA, CIPD, LLB

TRANSFORMING BUSINESS PERFORMANCE IN PRIVATE AND PUBLIC SECTORS

Felicia has worked in the Caribbean, U.K. and Africa. She is passionate about helping Nations build their competitiveness by transforming organisations in both the private and public sector. As an Organisational Transformation specialist she has a unique approach integrating governance, strategy and transformational capabilities such as culture and leadership. She has been owner and Director of Kitch Consulting and Coaching Ltd since its original incorporation in the Caribbean in 2007.

Felicia is both a technical specialist and a programme manager. She has led Technical Assistance teams on large scale transformation projects in the Caribbean and

Latin America, and, has implemented Technical Assistance Programmes for Governments in partnerships with donor agencies including the Inter-American Development Bank (IDB), Caribbean Development Bank (CDB), European Union (EU), Department for International Development (DFID) and the World Bank (WB). She has also designed and implemented private sector transformations in the Banking and Professional Services Sectors.

Projects she has led include; leading an EU funded Business Transformation Programme for the Government of the Turks and Caicos Islands improving key areas of service delivery such as work permits and business licencing, and supporting and facilitating the development of an Investment Policy White Paper and Stakeholder consultation; leading the DfID funded Public Sector Reform Programme for the Government of Montserrat where she spearheaded a project to develop a Policy Agenda that drove the Ministry strategies and aligned with the budget process. She also led a team of 10 consultants, both local and international, on a Public Expenditure Review for the Government of Barbados. This required a high level strategic review of 5 ministries and recommendations for redesigning Government structures to increase efficiency and effectiveness, which if implemented would yield substantial efficiency savings over a 3-year period. She has also been an evaluator for the Inter-American Development Bank assessing countries public sector management strategies to drive Development Results.

You may contact Felicia through her websites:

https://felicialinch.com/ and https://kitch-cc.com/

or her contact numbers:

UK +44 020 8177 1903 or Barbados: +1 246 830 6307

Made in the USA
Lexington, KY
15 November 2019